EVERYONE'S A CHANGE AGENT

EVERYONE'S A CHANGE AGENT

THE POWER OF WORDS
FOR BETTER – FOR WORSE

Nelson Price

Foreword by Terry Hershey

AVIVA
PUBLISHING
New York

EVERYONE'S A CHANGE AGENT
Nelson Price
All rights reserved.
Copyright © 2025 Nelson Price

ISBN #: 978-1-63618-411-1
Library of Congress Control Number: 2025919080
Published by:
Aviva Publishing
Lake Placid, NY
518-523-1320
www.avivapubs.com

Address all inquiries to:
NelsonPriceAuthor.com/contact-me

Layout and Design: Compass Rose Consulting, LLC
Cover Design: Compass Rose Consulting, LLC
https://compassroseconsulting.com

Nelson Price has captured in these pages how profound and real meaning can occur in the midst of everyday encounters. He makes us realize how even small and inconsequential events in our lives might at times be life changing for another. He is a gifted writer and storyteller who gets us to recognize and claim our own power to love. He is a man of deep faith and wisdom whose rich and varied life experiences are for the reader — form giving. Once started it is hard to put this spiritual guidebook down.

The Rev. Dr. Daniel P. Matthews Rector Emeritus Trinity Church Wall Street, New York City, NY

DEDICATION

To Barbara
For your love, friendship,
Companionship
Adventures
Our life together
Your love changed my life.

To my family
Four Children
Fifteen Grandchildren
Seven Great Grandchildren.
So much love

Table of Contents

FOREWORD

TERRY HERSHEY

In a world that too often feels upside down, we wonder, "What does it matter? Can I really make a difference?"

Nelson Price's answer is straightforward: Yes. We can make a difference.

And sometimes we need stories more than food to stay alive. Stories about profiles in courage, stories to remind us what really matters, and allow us to see with our heart. Everyone is a Change Agent, is a book of those stories, about people who made choices that led to transformational experiences that changed their lives, and the world around them.

Choices that made space for sanctuary, healing and growth,

and wisdom and renewal.

One of my favorite parts: change and transformation happen not because of a specific script or creed. There's not a test to pass. Change and transformation spills from a heart that is open and fully alive.

Yes, the power of choice. Viktor Frankl's reminder that "Everything can be taken from a man but one thing: the last of the human freedoms – to choose one's attitude in any given set of circumstances, to choose one's own way."

Jon Meacham said recently, "Courage is one of the most contagious things you can imagine."

It doesn't matter what we expect from life, but what life expects from us. In other words, we can choose.

We can choose to unbridle our heart, in order to be our better selves.

We can choose to release grief, to heal emotional wounds, and to open ourselves to transformation.

We can choose the gift and healing power of courage.

So, here's our question. How do we remind one another of the courage and sufficiency that is within us, when times are tough, dark and hurtful?

And how do we remember, even in the belittling and demanding places, that we can hear and affirm that voice of courage, and with it, walk one another home?

It is so easy (and tempting) to see our vulnerability as a weakness, or limitation or flaw, and not as the affirmation of a strong and resilient heart.

In this book, Nelson has created a useful "hat rack" to help us choose—a helpful way to name, and to focus, on what really matters in our capacity to make a difference in someone's life, and in the world around us. The invitation to choose to unleash the heart, in order to be our better selves.

Being a positive change agent is not always easy. And yet, speaking of people who made a transformational change, John Lewis left some awfully big shoes to fill, and gratefully, a word of encouragement along with advice about filling the shoes for being a change agent:

"Do not get lost in a sea of despair. Do not become bitter or hostile. Be hopeful, be optimistic. Never, ever be afraid to make some noise and get in good trouble, necessary trouble. We will find a way to make a way out of no way."

Today, we're invited to a paradigm shift. We often hear people say, "I know my rights," but seldom hear, "I know my responsibilities and obligations."

With no ego to protect, I can give my heart to create sanctuaries of kindness. To place love at the center.

And no one can take that away. They can demean us, belittle us, criticize us and silence us. But no one can take that away. So, today let us choose to speak the language of the heart. To give and to build. One choice at a time.

What about tomorrow? We can't control that.

What about reaction or public opinion? We can't control that.

What about acceptance? We can't control that.

And in the stories in this book, it is not about learning the "right technique." The change agents in these stories chose to "lean toward the whispers" of their heart.

Because they were made of stronger stuff? No. Because ordinary people can do extraordinary things.

Here's the other great affirmation in Nelson's book. We are on this journey of being positive change agents together.

In the course of a conversation, a friend said to me, 'Ar scáth a chéile a mhaireann na daoine.' Not being an Irish speaker, I asked her what it meant. She replied, 'In the shelter of each other the people live.' This proverb stirred deep within me; as I reflect on it, I continue to discover its profound, rich meaning, one that is for everyone, irrespective of language, place or race.

"We have to stop pretending we are individuals that can go it alone… I believe that if we turn to one another… let go of our judgments, become curious about each other, and take the risk to begin a conversation… the world will be a better place." (Thank you, Margaret J Wheatley, Turning to One Another)

We do make a difference in our world. And the choices we make do matter.

There are days when I need to hear Mr. Rogers' voice, "It's not so much what we have in this life that matters. It's what we do with what we have. The alphabet is fine, but it's what we do with it that matters most. Making words like 'friend' and 'love'. That's what really matters." (We could use more of Mr. Rogers in this world. Just sayin'.)

So, I wonder, how do we find the courage to choose what really matters?

What I do know is that each week I'm more aware of why struggles (anger or tears or sadness cropping up when I least expect them) make choices about what matters difficult. This is no surprise, with all the uncertainty and conflict in our world. I forget (or lose track) of the integrity of my inner Voice (what Marilynn Robinson called the "reservoir of goodness").

We've lost the empowerment that comes from knowing that what is at our core (compassion, generosity, kind-heartedness, our capacity for connection) is greater than whatever change confronts or challenges us. In other words, we have forgotten our best selves. We have forgotten that we were made for this, one soul helping another.

Yes, we get to choose the kind of world we want to live in. Let's begin with Helen Keller's reminder, "I am one, but still I am one; I cannot do everything, but still I can do something. And just because I cannot do everything, I will not refuse to do the something that I can do."

Taking Mother Teresa's words to heart, "If you can't feed a hundred people, then feed just one."

Bottom line: gratefully, indifference is not an option.

So. I can choose to be kind.

I can choose to be generous.

I can choose to be inclusive.

I can choose to not demean or shame.

I can choose to be a positive change agent.

This is not because we get points, or rewards in heaven. We can choose because this is a reflection of who we are, at our core. "This little light of mine, I'm gonna let it shine."

I love the work I do talking, teaching, entertaining. But, if I'm honest, there are times when I wonder why I still do "what" I do. I know that I have choices. But on my darker days I wonder, what difference can I really make?

Reading Nelson's book was an uplifting affirmation for me. And I'm so grateful. I can hear the skeptical part of me asking, "Can I really make a difference?"

And I see Nelson smiling, and hear him say, "Yes, my friend. You can."

This may be an old story. But I love telling it...As the old man walks the beach at dawn, he notices a young man picking up starfish and flinging them into the sea. Catching up to the youth, he asks a simple question, "Why are you doing this?' The boy answers that the stranded starfish would die if left until the morning sun.

Let us take Nelson's invitation today: Everyone is a Change Agent. Today, I can be an advocate for change, that is positive and affirmative. I can connect people and ideas and solutions that might never have crossed paths.

I can leave things better than I found them, with a smile and a kind word, making space for inclusion and justice, and investing in a world where we remember that we are indeed brother and sister.

PREFACE

Since you picked up this book, you are curious, interested in knowledge, and want to be a better person. You want to know how your actions and words may affect a child, teenager, spouse, friend or colleague.

My career was a Professional Communicator for a national organization: writer, speaker, producer of film, television, radio and documentaries. I sought to inform, motivate, and inspire readers, listeners and viewers. I was President and CEO of a cable network.

But it wasn't until I had a conversation with a person I did not know at a college event that I had a transformational experience, an aha moment. Our words can change a life, can save a life. That experience launched me on this journey.

This is an exploration of a *profound, provocative and new understanding* of how and why our words can change a person's core beliefs, outlook and behavior. Has a childhood "script" constricted your life, or has it encouraged freedom, exploration and a free spirit?

I believe in the power of stories. You will find stories about real events that move to the central thesis.

For you to know where the author is coming from, here is background information.

Biography

Nelson Price was a professional communicator all his career. He started out in radio and quickly moved to start a pilot public relations program for Methodist bishops.

He moved to the denomination's Television, Radio, and film Commission (TRAFCO) in Nashville, TN. where he produced radio and television programs for syndication and films and videos for use in local churches.

Price moved to New York City where he headed the Public Media Division of United Methodist Communications with responsibility for relating to television, radio and cable networks. His staff related to the Press and reported on events in the life of the denomination.

He was executive producer of the first national radio call-in program, Night Call, which was launched following the assassination of Martin Luther King, Jr. Cities were burning. violence was rampant. It aired at 11:30 p.m. to 12:30 a.m. Eastern time, 9:30 Western time.

The program brought listeners into dialogue with "movement" and national leaders. On heavy nights, over 40 thousand attempts were made to reach the program. Persons proclaimed, "I never talked to a Black person before." Or one of many national leaders on the program.

The Public Media Division, which Price headed, moved the Church into a concern for the effect television violence has on children, teenagers and adults. He was president of the newly created Media Action Research Center (MARC) and partnered with research professors at the State University of New York, Stony Brook, NY. The research team was headed by Dr. Robert M. Liebert, PhD. MARC created Television Awareness Training (TAT) to train teachers and leaders how to mitigate the negative effects of violent television programming.

Price and Dr. Liebert testified before Communications Committees of the Senate and House to show how a simple 30-second spot could influence six-year-olds to find positive ways to deal with conflict situations.

He was part of a White House Conference on Children and Television.

The last five years of his career, Price was president and CEO of the Odyssey Cable Network, a coalition of 67 denominations and faith organizations. The network hosted Nelson Mandela on his first visit to the United States, a huge celebration and service at Riverside Church in New York City. The network presented programs of faith, ethics, values and entertainment, all to be an instrument of positive change. Throughout Price's career, he witnessed how "word and image" could change people's lives.

Price received his bachelor's degree from Morningside College in Sioux City, Iowa, and his master's degree in psychology from Goddard College in Plainfield, Vermont. In this book, he reveals a new understanding of how change happens in our lives.

Foundational Beliefs and Approach

If you choose to journey with me on my road to discovery, and hopefully, new insights, there are several foundational beliefs from which I now come:

As a life-long Methodist, son of missionary parents and pastor, I approach Christian scripture in what Methodists call "The Wesleyan Quadrilateral." [1] It was developed by theologian Albert Outler from the writings of John Wesley, an Anglican priest and the British founder of Methodism world-wide. They are:

Scripture, the most important: The historical and Biblical Jesus is our example of how to live generously and justly.

Tradition: What is our faith tradition and what has it taught us? John Wesley, the founder of the many Methodist and Wesleyan movements in the U.S. and around the world, was a Church of England priest. On May 24, 1738, he recorded in his diary an experience which changed his life and energized his ministry. It was transformational.

"In the evening, I went very unwillingly to a society in Aldersgate Street, where one was reading [Martin] Luther's preface to the Epistle to the Romans. About a quarter before nine, while he was describing the change which God works in the heart through faith in Christ, I felt my heart strangely

---

[1] "Glossary: Wesleyan Quadrilateral." United Methodist Communications. The United Methodist Church, April 15, 2025. https://www.umc.org/en/content/glossary-wesleyan-quadrilateral-the.

warmed. I felt I did trust in Christ, Christ alone, for salvation; and an assurance was given me that He had taken away my sins, even mine, and saved me from the law of sin and death"[2]

He did not intend to start denominations but simply, a holiness movement that included everyone.

Reason: It makes sense. Some of the reported Biblical practices no longer make sense: the clothing we wear, not eating pork, an "eye for an eye," natural disasters are caused by God as ipunishment. God uses wars as a vehicle to move the "kingdom" closer. We bring reason to understanding the scriptures.

Experience: Our own experience of our faith journey. Perhaps, when our hearts are "strangely warmed." When we experience "God moments" of awe. Or an "aha" moment of discovery. When we experience love – it is a "God experience" for "God is love" and when we experience genuine love, we are experiencing the Holy.

1. God, by whatever name we may use, continues to be revealed to us. God did not stop speaking to humankind at the end of the third century. Otherwise, why would we pray?
2. Our understanding of God may change. For example, how God continues to create and to enter our human condition as it is right now, not as it was 2000 years ago. And we are co-creators with God in making a better world.

---

[2] Joe Iovino, "Holy Spirit Moments: Learning from Wesley at Aldersgate, The United Methodist Church, April 30, 2025, https://www.umc.org/en/content/holy-spirit-moments-learning-from-wesley-at-aldersgate .

3. Christianity does not have a "corner" on God or Jesus. Christians see Jesus as an example of how to live. God's revelation in Jesus belongs to everyone. God's revelation to anyone belongs to everyone. Peter said, as recorded in Acts 10:34-35 (GW): "Now I understand that God doesn't play favorites. [35] Rather, whoever respects God and does what is right is acceptable to him in any nation."

4. In writing and speaking, I try to differentiate between beliefs, thoughts, and feelings. Often, we mix them up.

   a. I *believe* Jesus is an example of how we should live.

   b. I *think* our planet is at risk.

   c. I *feel* scared of what the future holds for our children and grandchildren.

   d. Sometimes we have an intuition, but we can't get a rational handle on it. It is close to a feeling and may be a nudge by God. It may be worth acting on.

I often hear, "I'm feeling we need to…" when they really "think" we should do whatever. A "feeling" is an emotion: happy, sad, hopeful, fearful. But saying "I feel" rather than "I think" or "I believe" may seem softer and more likely to be accepted, or less of a certainty, more tentative.

Why Me?

I struggled with the audacity of thinking I had something that might be helpful to others. A lay person. Not a biblical scholar. Not a trained theologian. Is it truly helpful? But it kept nagging at me. I heard messages that said, "Risk. Don't be afraid. You have a responsibility to share your beliefs. They may help someone."

I was encouraged by Choctaw elder and retired Episcopal Bishop Steven Charleston who writes about how prophets arise in periods of crisis or apocalypse to chart a message of resilience and hope:

"I invite you to join me in becoming a prophet…it does not matter what your race or religion might be. It does not matter what age or gender you are. We can all become prophets in our own time. We are all needed…" [3]

Certainly, I don't see myself as a prophet. But my faith, my personal and professional experiences coalesced in my consciousness with power and urgency.

Michelle Obama captures it best for me in her book, *The Light We Carry*. She writes:

I believe that each of us carries a bit of inner brightness, something entirely unique and individual, a flame that's worth protecting. When we are able to recognize our own light, we become empowered to use it. [4]

And finally, the scripture Matthew 5:15: "Neither do men light a lamp, and put it under the bushel, but on the stand; and it shineth unto all that are in the house."

[3] Steven Charleston, *We Survived the End of the World* (Broadleaf Books, 2023).
[4] Michelle Obama, *The Light We Carry* (Crown, 2022), 16.

ONE

CHANGE

Everyone is a change agent – whether we intend to be or not, for good or for worse, by word and by action. We have a choice of what we say or do. We do not have a choice on what is heard or interpreted.

The author came to this insight through personal experience in his professional life. as a communications officer for the United Methodist Church, a television, radio and film producer, his study of psychology and research on the effects of television on children and adults. His life purpose was to create messages that affirmed the "good" in people and to motivate them into a deeper faith and participation in making our world a better place.

This exploration is not "how to find happiness." It's not "therapy."

It's about "transformation" and how it takes place. It's about "awareness" of your power to change lives – to hurt or to heal. It's about understanding the negative messages you live with and may pass on to others. It's about the traumas buried deeply in your core being. Recognizing them may help you to "de-fang and to disable" them, to free you from their harmful effects.

A change agent can be of any age.

Montgomery

In March 1955, Montgomery, Alabama was tense. Buses were segregated. Blacks in back. Whites in front. A 15-year-old girl rode the bus to school each day.

One day she decided she was not going to give up her seat to a white woman. The police arrested her, dragged her off the bus, and took her to jail.

The "movement" did not anticipate her action. Claudette Colvin was too young, unwed, and pregnant. The Montgomery white press and the white power structure would destroy her. They didn't want her to be the "face" of the protest.

Nine months later, Rosa Parks, secretary of the local chapter of the National Association for the Advancement of Colored People (NAACP) and a trained civil rights protester, refused to give up her seat to a white rider.

It launched the boycott of Black riders on public buses. They organized carpools to substitute for the bus system. Bus ridership dropped dramatically, bringing financial pressure on the system.

Colvin was still a part of the legal process. She was one of four plaintiffs in the federal court case. She testified. The case went all the way to the Supreme Court.

The result: the Supreme Court found that the laws authorizing segregated buses to be unconstitutional and later, that all public transportation must be desegregated.

It was a profound win for justice and equal protection under the law. It started a civil rights revolution led by The Rev. Dr. Martin Luther King, Jr.

A 15-year-old schoolgirl started a civil rights revolution. Our actions can make a difference. [5]

Another teenager who changed the world

Darnella Frazier was walking along a Minneapolis street on May 25, 2020, when she came upon a police scene. A police officer was holding down a Black man who was struggling to survive. His name was George Floyd.

Darnella, a 17-year-old Black American, grabbed her cell phone and began recording the event. The video went viral. It was used in court to convict the police officer. It started a new accountability for police officers. It changed training for police departments across the country. It spawned protests across the country. The video went around the world!

Darnella even received an honorary Pulitzer Prize. In reflecting on her action, she said, "Even though this was a

---

[5] "Claudette Colvin," Wikipedia, Wikimedia Foundation, Inc., April 10, 2025. https://en.wikipedia.org/wiki/Claudette Colvin

traumatic life-changing experience for me, I'm proud of myself. If it weren't for my video, the world wouldn't have known the truth."

But there was a price to pay for Danella. It also changed her life – the trauma of seeing a man killed.

"Everyone talks about the girl who recorded George Floyd's death, but to actually be her is a different story," she wrote. "My video didn't save George Floyd," she added, "but it put his murderer away and off the streets." [6]

A Change of Heart

Jamie Bruesehoff recounts the journey she and her pastor husband made in parenting a child beyond the binary. It was apparent at an early age that their son was drawn to feminine clothes, colors, and behavior. When the kindergarten teacher first asked the children to line up as boys and girls, he went to the girls' line.

Jamie and her husband did not stop loving him. They didn't criticize or try to change him. He was their child. They loved him as he grew and figured out who he was.

She said, "Helping our children negotiate their own preferences versus the anticipated reactions of the people around them (and the potential safety concerns that come with those people) is not simple."

---

[6] Errin Haines. "Darnella Frazier, the teen who filmed George Floyd's murder, wins honorary Pulitzer." The 19th*, The 19th News. June 11, 2021.
https://19thnews.org/2021/06/darnella-frazier-teen-filmed-george-floyds-murder-wins-honorary-pulitzer/

It's a long journey from birth to eight years old. They decided he could "come out" to the congregation at age eight in a worship service.

Jamie writes that she was tense and apprehensive when Rebecca came out. After the service, she saw a man heading for her husband who was greeting worshipers as they left the sanctuary. The person had a reputation for strong opinions and a willingness to share them.

He said to his pastor, "Listen, I don't understand this whole transgender thing…But she used to hide behind your wife's skirts and not answer me when I said 'hi'. And today? Today, she ran up to me, twirled in her dress, and gave me a high-five." Jamie reports, "He shrugged. 'What more is there to know?'"

Not a word was used. No arguments trying to change his point of view. No sermons changed his view. No scripture. But a blossoming youngster, free and happy, changed his belief. [7]

Non-Verbal Communication

We also communicate nonverbally. A frown, smile, lifted eyebrow, grimace. A fist, a slap, push, kick. An adult or parent's, "The Look." Our body posture may communicate confidence, fearfulness, hesitancy, cautiousness, bashfulness. Or our posture may communicate confidence, at home in our "skin" and who we are.

We communicate when we show up at concerts, sports events, restaurants, bars, worship services. We volunteer for worthy

[7] Jamie Bruesehoff, *Raising Kids Beyond the Binary* (Broadleaf Books, 2023), xvi & xvii .

projects, attend rallies in support or opposition to causes. It's a statement.

There are many ways, besides words that we communicate.

Why Words?

Our focus is on "words," because we use words every day. Words bombard us from television, radio, and film. So much wisdom is recorded in the printed word, including holy scriptures. Words are an ever-present reality in our lives.

But more than that. Words are core to human existence and experience. The development of language and the ability to write may be the greatest achievement in human history. They allow us to communicate with each other and to store knowledge in books, libraries and digitally. Words are the basis of our knowledge and our relationships.

It is often said that "action is stronger than words," but many times words come before action. Words embody ideas that motivate action.

I think we all recognize the power of words by leaders like Martin Luther King, Jr. The Pope. The Bible. Kuran. The president. The scholars of holy scriptures. We recognize the power of their words, *but don't recognize the power of our words*. We look at *them* as "thought shaping" leaders. But this book is about the power everyone has and why our words are so powerful.

While I come to this conversation from a Christian perspective, I believe persons of most faith traditions can relate to it.

Personal Reflection & Notes:

TWO

THE WORD IN SCRIPTURE

The **Word** was very important and central to Jewish and Christian thought as described in their Holy Scriptures.

The creation story in Genesis describes the creation of the world. In every translation of the Bible, the language is: (Genesis 1:3), "And God said, 'Let there be light,' and there was light." (English Standard version). Or "God spoke: "'Light!' And light appeared." (The Message.) God "spoke," and it was done. As creation of our world progressed in the Genesis account, in every translation, it began, "And God said…," or a slight variation, and "it is good..." And God said, and God said, and God said. And the whole world was created.

The writers of Genesis envisioned the world as being created

9

by "the **Word**." They saw great power in God's word.

We now understand more clearly how the world evolved and was created, perhaps, how God did it. Whatever our belief, we live in a marvelous creation. But creation is not static. God, by whatever name you call this tremendous power, continues to create. Creation is a living, changing, inter-connected, complicated miracle. So far, our earthly home is the only known planet like ours in the universe.

Now, we are creating the world we live in through words of love and words of hate.

The Word Became Flesh

In the New Testament, John in his Gospel, also related "the Word" to God and God's power. In John 1:1, the Revised Standard Version (RSV) of the Bible, the writer says, *"In the beginning was the Word, and the Word was with God, and the Word was God."*

And then in John 1:14: "And the Word became flesh and dwelt among us, full of grace and truth; we have beheld his glory, glory as of the only Son from the Father."

Christians call this "the Incarnation." It simply means, Jesus came into the world through God's Word as God's son.

Encyclopedia Britannica defines incarnation this way:

Incarnation, a central Christian doctrine that God became flesh, that God assumed a human nature_and became a man in the form of Jesus Christ, the Son of God and the second person of the Trinity. Christ was truly God and truly human.[8]

In his book **The Universal Christ**, Catholic theologian, scholar and founder of the Center for Action and Contemplation, Richard Rohr proposes that Jesus is for everyone; that Christ's dying on the cross is for all humanity, not just for His followers. His dying and rising free us all to live as Jesus lived – the "good life." Jesus' sacrifice was for all humanity – past, present, future. [9] Jesus is not exclusive to Christians.

Franciscan sister Ilia Delio focuses on the theology of the incarnation and the universal nature of the Christ mystery. She writes:

"The Christian message is that God has become flesh [sarx in Greek or "matter"]—not a part of God or one aspect of God but the whole infinite, eternal God Creator has become matter. The claim—God has become flesh—is so radical that it is virtually unthinkable and illogical. Christianity is the most radical of all world religions because it takes matter seriously as the home of divinity." [10]

The Christian faith is *"so radical"* that WORDS become our reality – we live on a holy planet created by God's Word.

Radical – that God came to live amongst us as Jesus, the Christ to *show us* how to live and how to love; how to accept everyone as brothers and sisters; how to love our neighbor and even our

[8] Editors, Encyclopedia Britannica, "Incarnation," Britannica, Accessed April 15, 2025. https://www.britannica.com/topic/Christianity/The-problem-of-scriptural-authority.
[9] Rohr, Richard, The Universal Christ: How a Forgotten Reality Can Change Everything We See, Hope For, and Believe (Convergent Books, 2019.

[10] Ilia Delio, "Christogenesis by Any Other Name?," Center for Christogenesis, October 12, 2020, https://christogenesis.org/christogenesis-by-any-other-name.

enemy, how to give and how to forgive.

The word "incarnation" is not in our normal vocabulary. We don't think about it until Christmas when Christians celebrate Jesus' birth as the "incarnation of God" in human form, to teach us, show us who God is.

So, what is new?

We thought the incarnation ended with Jesus. It didn't.

Our Words also can become incarnate in another person and transform that person's life into a radical new direction. When our "word" enters deeply into the psyche, mind and soul of another person, their life is turned into a different direction. First the incarnation of our words into the flesh of another person, then a transformation.

We are created in God's image. Genesis 1:27 states, "So God created man (humans) in his own image, in the image of God created he him; male and female created he them."

We have been given great power.

When our word becomes flesh, becomes "incarnate" in another -- a child, a teenager, an adult-- it radically changes what they believe and how they behave. They have a new reality, a new life. Our word becomes "flesh" by being incarnate in another person's "flesh."

For good – or for bad. For health or for harm. For joy or for anger.

This is the core thesis of this book. Our words can become "incarnate" in another person, and this incarnation is so radical it changes that person's life. This is the God-power we have been given.

Personal Reflection & Notes:

THREE

THE POWER OF CHANGE

In the Gospel of Matthew 10:1 we read, "Jesus summoned His twelve disciples and gave them authority over unclean spirits, to cast them out, and to heal every kind of disease and every kind of sickness."

The power of our words to be incarnational can heal and dismiss the unclean spirits that prevent us from becoming what God intended us to be. It can change our script. It can even "move mountains" – the mountains of hate, anger, prejudice, vengefulness, fear, the need for power, control or pride.

Father Richard Rohr writes:

"There is not a single discipline studied today that does not recognize change, development, growth, and some kind of evolving phenomenon: psychology, cultural anthropology, history, physical sciences, philosophy, social studies, art, drama, music, on and on. But in theology's search for the Real Absolute, it made one fatal mistake. It imagined a static "unmoved mover," as Aristotelian philosophy called it, a solid substance sitting above somewhere." [11]

Change, yes. But the incarnational God gave us the power to affect change for the better. In this way, we are co-creators with God

I believe that everyone who is doing good – is doing God's will. And, of course, the opposite is also true. This belief opens me to appreciate and to accept the overwhelming goodness of people, regardless of their faith or identity. We are all one in creating the GOOD – God's will for us.

There are two types of changes to consider:

1. Changes that do not change our core, incarnate beliefs.

   When I was married, it radically changed my life, but it did not change my belief in love and the power of love.

   When I moved from one city to another, it did not change my beliefs, but it radically changed my life.

   When I changed jobs, it did not change my beliefs, but it changed my life.

   When a word or an event or an experience becomes "incarnate," it changes one's belief, their sense of who

---

[11] Richard Rohr, "Evolving Faithfully," Center for Action and Contemplation. July 7, 2024, https://cac.org/daily-meditations/evolving-faithfully.

they are, and their behavior.

2. Incarnate, *life-changing* beliefs are described in various ways: an "aha" moment, a new insight, an epiphany, an awakening, a conversion, a discovery, a revelation, a spiritual awakening, born again, and more. They are buried deeply in our psyches, recognized and often unrecognized.

   For example, a friend had a bad experience on her first airplane flight. She doesn't fly any more.

   A friend had a near-drowning experience when she was eight. She continues to fear the water.

   A veteran had extreme war experiences. Now he won't go to places where there are crowds.

   PTSD – Post Traumatic Stress Disorder – affects the behavior and lives of many – traumas from many different sources.

A friend recommended the book "I'm Ok—You're Ok" by Dr. Thomas Harris, MD. It changed my life. It describes the discipline of Transactional Analysis for therapy and interpersonal relationships. I became an accredited practitioner for applications within organizations.

A clue to our hidden trauma is to look at what we avoid.

Again, each of us knows the power of words – to heal or to wound, to inform or to mislead, to tell the truth or to lie, to entertain or to frighten, to subdue or to free, to demean or to encourage. When our words become incarnate as a deep-seated belief, it changes our lives and how we become the person God intended us to be -- *or to fall short because of our negative beliefs in who we are.*

Our deep seated, positive incarnate beliefs that guide our lives may include –

> All people are made in God's image—everyone.
>
> Faith in God, by whatever words you use to capture that power.
>
> Acceptance of all people.
>
> Kindness.
>
> Inclusion.
>
> Unconditional love of family.
>
> Hard work.
>
> All work can contribute to the common good.
>
> Love is the power to "move mountains."
>
> Creating a world of justice and equal opportunity.

Richard Rohr's book, "The Universal Christ," was incarnated into my psyche and soul. It changed my life, my beliefs, and my seeing a more inclusive humanity. There are no "others." We are in this together. Christians don't exclusively "own" Christ.

What are your core values?

Personal Reflection & Notes:

FOUR

OUR PSYCHÈS

Words are powerful. Words change lives. We know that. We see it. Sometimes it seems that everyone wants us to change our thinking, our beliefs, our actions. To persuade us to their causes, to their political positions, to their faith beliefs. To buy their products, their medications, their services. They come from many sources: Advertising. Film. TV. Speeches. Self-help books. Internet. I-phone. Scripture. Sermons. The list is endless. Words come at us from all directions.

It may seem strange to write again about an obvious truth, that Words are powerful and affect us in different ways: our moods, our feelings, our self-worth, our beliefs, our behavior. Often Words that affect us most deeply may be spoken by a parent, sibling, friend, co-worker. But they also may come from teachers, preachers, political leaders as well as from television shows, movies, books, speeches, and advertising.

They are both positive and negative. Each of us has been hurt by someone else's words. "You're not college material." "You're not musical." "You don't have a voice good enough for chorus." "You're not athletic." "You're not mechanical." "You're dumb." "You're a nobody."

We also have been encouraged by the love of parents, siblings, friends, family. Words of affirmation and confirmation. Deposited there are even the family and cultural norms of past generations, both positive and negative.

These beliefs and experiences are buried deeply in our psyches, where all our human qualities are stored. Imagine an expandable balloon somewhere in your body that can stretch as more and more is stored. What is the balance between positive healthy traits and negative harmful traits? What traits are motivating your actions?

What is stored in our psyches affects us every day. They can be available to us. It just takes a trigger to bring a memory, an experience, an event, a person, a musical piece, a food — whatever is in our psyches can become available with the right trigger. It often can be surprising.

Words and Children

The *words* we use with children often become *incarnate* and stay with them for a lifetime. Words used by parents, peers, teachers, older siblings, peers, neighbors, adult authority figures are especially powerful. Children are constantly trying to figure out how their world works. It is these negative voices and beliefs that keep therapists in business.

Small children, adolescents and teenagers are curious and constantly looking for clues as to how the world works. A simple example: My four-year-old granddaughter was sitting on my lap. She was looking up at my face and saw it from a different angle. She asked, "Grandpa, why do you have hair in your nose and your ears?" I replied," To keep the bugs out." It made sense. That's how it works.

What is deposited in a child's psyche the first five years of their lives will guide them the rest of their lives, often creating a "script" to follow until it is interrupted.

What are some of these messages?

For example, I grew up during the Great Depression. Money was scarce. That scarcity was seared into my psyche so that it still is a part of my concerns over money.

Positive words can motivate children to try new things. They may affirm them in something they've done, learned or achieved.

"You are amazing!"

"You are very gifted."

"You're smart!"

"You can do it!"

"You are so athletic, musical, talented, generous, caring.

Negative messages to children can become embedded in their psyches and control their future lives.

"You're too dumb to do that."

"You're not college material."

"You're not athletic, or musical, or skilled."

"Abusive acts such as slapping, hitting, physically punishing."

"Don't be so stingy."

Children are not consciencely asking these questions, but they may be there.

"Is it safe in my home?"

"Are the adults in my home trustworthy and dependable?"

"Is it safe in my school and with my teacher?"

"Is it safe in my neighborhood? "Mom, can I go out and play?" Mom: "No honey, it's not safe. I'll take you out later."

"Do mommy and daddy love me?"

"Who scares me?"

"Do someone's words hurt me?"

"Am I bullied – by peers or adults?"

These "demons" -- Jesus cast out demons -- can be cast out through faith, stronger counter-messages, transformational experiences, therapy or self-discovery and realization.

This does not mean we don't offer constructive criticism, given in love, to help children learn and grow. Children also need to learn how to deal with failure.

Affirmation can come from many sources: books, music, art, worship, nature, scripture, and many more. It fills our psyches with a positive, affirming self-image that affects the way we believe and behave. They help us have good relationships, be successful, and be a positive influence on others and our society. To make our world a better place.

War Trauma

A rugged man "burst" into Dr. Edward Tick's office, psychotherapist for military personnel. He was "wearing a black leather riding jacket, tight jeans, and high black boots." He looked around the room, checked every door, then moved his chair into a corner where he could survey the entire room

Dr. Tick came out from behind his desk, took a chair facing the soldier. He had no paper pad. Art was surprised. "Not gonna scribble notes or nothin'?" He'd seen many therapists. Tick replied, "No, this meeting is just for us to get to know each other."

Art had trouble sleeping. He dreamed of war, enemy soldiers storming his position. He trusted no one. He experienced survivor's guilt, seeing both what he was doing in the present and his horrific war experiences. He had double vision.

Dr. Tick, after several interchanges: "You must have been frightened down to your very soul."

The word "soul" touched a raw wound. Art replied, he had lost his soul and knows exactly where & when. He was escaping a fierce bombardment when his soul left his body. There was much discussion about Art's wartime experiences, soul, and all souls.

Dr. Tick finally asked, "where is your soul now?" It was next to him, "trying to figure out whether to trust" Dr. Tick.

Art asked whether Dr. Tick thought he could get his soul back. Dr. Tick thought so, when the soul felt safe. The route to recovery had begun. [12]

PBS aired a documentary in which Dr. Tick reunited U.S. and Vietnam soldiers, an experience of reconciliation and forgiveness.

Our Darker Psyche

But there also is the darker side. When we fill our psyches with misinformation (inaccurate but not intentional) and disinformation (intentionally inaccurate), they create an alternate world view that also changes our beliefs and our actions. Social platform algorithms determine what we are fed and feed us more of the positive or negative platforms we choose, further leading us into a different reality. If we come to believe –

That others who are different from us are a danger to us and our identity

That minorities will overwhelm our white culture

That our federal government is a "swamp" and a threat to us

That all politicians are crooked and self-serving

If liberals or conservatives believe that "the other" is evil, it may give permission to commit violent or abusive acts against them, and when joined by millions, society changes.

As our psyches are devoted more and more with a distorted view of reality, it opens the door of reacting in violent, sexist, and racist ways.

We witness violence every day: Charlottesville where a car

---

[12] Edward Tick, War and the Soul: Healing our Nation's Veterans from Post-traumatic Stress Disorder (Quest Books, 2005).

crashed into a crowd of demonstrators, killing a young woman. The attack on the Tree of Life Synagogue in Pittsburgh, killing eleven. Mass shootings affect millions of school children and their families. The Timothy McVeigh bombing of a federal building in Oklahoma City. The shoe bomber, whose effect was to make billions of air travelers take off their shoes. The shooting of a company president on the street in New York City in broad daylight moved other business leaders to consider installing protective measures. There will be many more examples as we move into the future.

The White Supremist Movement seeks to spread terror and fear. Their strategy is to energize "lone wolf" or "vigilante" attacks. The carnage in the U.S is unprecedented.

There are many consequences. Children fear going to school. Schools are locked and have security officers. Houses of worship are locked. Some have guards. Security at airports and office buildings has changed our lives. Security cameras everywhere. The security industry is booming.

One leader said, "To make America Great Again, we need to make America White Again." Targets are Jews, gays, trans, immigrants and persons of color. White men are encouraged to "unite and fight."

White Supremists "welcome the chaos." Their goal: to make "American white again." [13]

White Christian Nationalism proposes we should be guided by their interpretation of the Bible and incorporated it into our

---

[13] Richard Rowley, director/writer, *Documenting Hate: New American Nazis*, Season 2018, Episode 17, Frontline. Aired November 3, 2020 on PBS, https://www.youtube.com/watch?v=-XFBVAAzXjc.

government policies and programs. By its nature, it would harm persons and institutions of other faiths.

Healthy Incarnate Beliefs

Every faith -- every religion – leads us and encourages us to be better human beings. They motivate us to care for and love each other. Jesus entreaties us to "love our neighbor as ourselves."

The golden rule in Buddhism is known as the *"Golden Rule of Reciprocity" or the "Law of Karma."* We reciprocate to another as we would like them to treat us. Sahih Muslim, Book 1, Number 72 reads, *"None of you has faith until he loves for his brother or his neighbor what he loves for himself."*

There are so many people and hundreds of organizations working to improve the lives of people – to create a better world. We are a nation of volunteers. There is hope.

Faith communities have built hospitals, colleges and universities, community centers, justice movements, drug treatment centers, programs to assist the poor, hungry and homeless. Civic organizations work to create positive change.

Throughout our history, we have worked to make our society and democracy more just. As recently as 1974, women couldn't get a credit card. They couldn't build a credit record and therefore couldn't borrow money for an education, to own a home, to build a business, to be independent. They literally were captive to their husbands.

Our healthy and unhealthy beliefs become a part of who we are through the words and examples of parents, teachers, holy scriptures, books, pastors/priests/imams, internet, political messaging, so many sources!

Harmful Incarnate Beliefs

There are deeply held beliefs we may hold that are harmful to ourselves, our families, our communities, our country and the world. No small thing.

We live in a culture where there is a war between truth and misinformation. Powerful and well-funded sources are interested in gaining power, wealth and prevailing in their vision for the future.

There is a movement whose strategy is simple: destroy the trust in our institutions, deny, spread misinformation, create think tanks to support their views, own television, radio, cable, – the media. AI (Artificial Intelligence) makes it more difficult to tell truth from falsehood with its ability to create believable false messages from reputable individuals, organizations and governments.

Their purpose? To gather *power* to control the economy and the government to enrich themselves. The forces of power, greed and oppression are still rampant, threatening democracies, care for our planet, care for all human life, and so much more.

Beginning in 2025 with a new administration, democracy began to rapidly change. Laws were ignored. Tens of thousands of people were fired. Government agencies were gutted. Thousands of contracts were cancelled. Aid programs to developing countries were cancelled, affecting the health and food sources for hundreds of thousands of people. If sustained, millions of children and adults will die.

The easiest way to get people to follow them is through fear - - to frighten them – to create a "culture of fear."

Make everyone fearful of retribution if they oppose their actions: loss of job, physical harm to immediate and extended family.

Blame refugees for crime and taking jobs. An underlying message is people of color are taking over and threatening the white population and its majority.

Don't believe scientists. "There has always been climate change; it's natural." So, we don't need to do anything to mitigate the warming of the oceans, the warming of the atmosphere, the most severe hurricanes and fires. We can keep on burning fossil fuels.

But no matter how much change and its causes are denied, reality eventually wins.

"Isms" are buried in our psyches and affect our beliefs, our words and our actions. The "ism" of racism is buried deeply in many individuals and also in our society – systemic racism. Homophobia seeks to harm and deny a person's sexuality. Classism, antisemitism, sexism and so many other isms. Fear creates "the other," persons unlike us. They become the enemy.

Are liberals negative about evangelicals or conservatives? Do I stereotype someone who wears a cross? Do I prejudge persons who protest at abortion clinics? Do I look down on people who wear a MAGA hat?

Experiences of war, rape, abuse as a child negatively affect their lives until they are healed.

If our life goals are to improve and to change, we want to reduce the space taken up by negative, harmful characteristics in our psychic storeroom to space occupied by healthy and loving characteristics.

If you want to heal your "isms," ask yourself, "What do I fear? What do I believe?"

> Do I cross the street to avoid a person different from me?
>
> Do I become angry when I disagree with another person over an issue?
>
> Do I fear our country may become a majority of people of color?
>
> Do I believe a man can do a job better than a woman?
>
> Do I believe X is an inferior race?
>
> Do I believe my way is the only way?

In addition, you might ask about other fears. What causes my fear of…heights, speaking in public, women, men, gays, trans. What is keeping me from accepting people who are different from me as they are? What do I avoid?

The first step is to look at facts, whether it is still true, what is best for making our world better, what information do I need? What is the loving thing to do? What kind of person do I want to be?

There has been exhaustive evaluation and opinion on the results of the 2024 presidential and congressional elections. The election will be studied for years to come. The fact is, those who voted made an enormous decision which changed the course of history. What a U.S. president decides on issues like climate change affects every human, animal and plant in the world, not just the U.S. Our voices matter. Our words matter. Our actions matter.

Personal Reflection & Notes:

FIVE

MY JOURNEY OF DISCOVERY

My journey to the revelation of the broader meaning of *incarnation* was through many personal, professional and faith experiences. I hope they will trigger similar experiences for you and help you recognize God's gift to you of power and witness.

"Go to Hell"

When I was five years old, my church had a week of "vacation Bible School." It was a time when children of the congregation gathered for Christian education. There were about 35 young people from very young to teens sitting on the church lawn. The last night, we were gathered to hear a lesson by a "chalk talk artist." The artist told a Biblical story while drawing with colored chalk on a large pad the scene of the story.

We were all enraptured as the picture emerged. He talked about "heaven and hell," how horrible hell is, and who would go there. There was the angry, fierce-faced devil with his long spear, people screaming and suffering and burning in a "hell hole," and angels were looking down on it all.

His last words were, "If someone tells someone else to go to hell, that person won't go, but the person who told him—will! I had never thought of heaven or hell or telling someone to go to hell. But a couple of weeks later, I was so frustrated and angry with my older sister, I told her to "go to hell." She replied gleefully, "Ha, ha, ha. I'm not going. You are!"

I was devastated. I went to bed crying. My mother came up to console me and to find out why I was sobbing so deeply. I could not tell her. And my sister did not reveal the secret, either.

That "word" became "incarnate" and a part of my life view, my self-image, and a fear of a judgmental, score-keeping God. It took years to change that incarnate belief to understanding that Christ had died to forgive me (and you and all humankind) and that God loved me, regardless.

A believer who comes to belief through fear rather than love is a superficial believer. Imagine trying to get someone to love you by making them afraid of you. Children should not be afraid of their parents.

For centuries, fear was a motivating force to bring people into the Church. The fear of hell, purgatory, God's judgement. It brought people in. They volunteered and gave their money. Many found faith. It created an institution and hierarchy, mostly positive, sometimes negative.

You Saved My Life

In mid-career, I took a sabbatical to study for a master's degree in psychology with an emphasis on Transactional Analysis. It was the mid-70's and Transactional Analysis (TA) was popularized by the best-selling book by Dr. Thomas Harris, *"I'm OK -- You're OK."*

Transactional Analysis was developed by Dr. Eric Berne, M.D., and a psychiatrist, as a discipline for use in psychotherapy. Berne's most famous book was *"Games People Play,"* psychological games with catchy names. For instance, NIGYYSOB (Now I've got you, you son-of-a-bitch) catching someone who may have made a misstep. IWFY (If it weren't for you) often played between spouses, or ITHY (I'm only Trying to Help You), along with many others. The book was on the New York Time's best seller list for months. First published in July 1964, by October 1966 it had been reprinted 26 times.

Transactional Analysis proposes that each of us operates out of three ego states: Parent, Adult, and Child. When we are interacting with another person, it is a transaction. The Parent might be critical or nurturing. The Child might be angry and hurt, or joyful and playful. The Adult ego state is where we are communicating truthfully, with facts and problem solving. Many of us now recognize the "child" in us but not the "parent" or "adult."

In therapy, the transactions are analyzed and exposed, where they can be acknowledged and dealt with. For example, when a person's Critical Parent may be scolding, the other person may hear that transaction with their hurt child. I think all of us hear the "critical parent" or adult in our childhoods giving us instructions.

This oversimplification may "tease" you to explore more. Berne wrote several books including "Group Treatment," "Sex in Human Loving," and "Transactional Analysis in Psychotherapy." Other psychotherapists have written dozens of books that apply Transactional Analysis to different settings: "The OK Boss" by James, "Games Alcoholics Play" by Steiner, and "Games Students Play" by Ernst.

I chose Goddard College because of its progressive philosophy and its flexible study program. It is an early model of a much more common educational program today. I could stay at home and be with my young family.

There were on campus symposia for all graduate students during the year. We shared our work and progress. It was at these sessions where I had an "aha" insight.

I was late for lunch in the cafeteria. There was only one other person in the line. I asked if she'd like to have lunch together, and she readily agreed. We found a table in a corner away from a few lingering students. I don't remember a lot about the conversation. I remember it was pleasant. I'm sure we shared our study programs. I was enthusiastic about my focus, and I think I must have shared with her some of my experiences with Transactional Analysis and its basic concepts.

After a longish lunch we said goodbye and didn't bump into each other again during that symposium.

At the next symposium a few months later, she singled me out and asked if we could have lunch. We found a table away from others. The first thing she said was, **"You saved my life!"** I was stunned and simply waited for her to continue. "When we were together at the last symposium, I had decided to commit suicide. My daughter was estranged. I was alone. I couldn't see my granddaughter…" She paused.

"And now?" I questioned, waiting.

"Now my daughter and I have reconciled. We have found love and respect for each other. It's a good relationship, and I love being with my granddaughter."

I was blown away. I had no idea what I said could have turned her around.

But it also changed me. It was an epiphany, the incarnation and then the transformation. My beliefs had changed. It launched me on my investigation of the power of words.

I also learned we usually DON'T KNOW HOW OUR WORDS WILL AFFECT SOMEONE OR CHANGE THEIR LIVES. Eric Berne observed early in his practice, "We don't know when a word or a phrase or a sentence will change someone's life."

We are "change agents" whether we intend to be, or not. For better or for worse. We can nourish and encourage; we can diminish and demean. Both can affect lives. Our words can be heard and internalized so deeply (become incarnate) that they affect another person for the rest of their lives.

Surprise!

At one point that year, I videotaped a group therapy session with eight participants. When all had completed their struggles, we went back around and showed each their individual times on camera. The camera catches the whole person, unlike a mirror. It records body language, facial expressions, fidgety hands, posture. It can be quite sobering and a little scary.

When we came to a young woman, she sat up straighter and said, surprised, "I'm rather attractive." She didn't know that. At some time, she had received a negative message, and she believed it. It became incarnate. What an "aha" wonderful revelation and affirmation. I think it changed her life.

One person in the group was a retired military officer. When the video ended his session, his surprise was, "No wonder people are stand-offish." He could see his posture and demeanor were off-putting. What worked in his military life was not working as a civilian. It was a positive discovery which he could change. An "aha" moment.

Personal Reflection & Notes:

SIX

OTHER PEOPLE'S
CHANGE EXPERIENCES

I asked several people to share their experiences of incarnational change. Perhaps they will trigger new insights for you, your own "aha" moment.

Expectations

From our earliest memories, there are expectations of us to perform at levels of excellence, to receive enchiladas for a job well done, and to be rewarded accordingly. For some of us those high standards seemed impossible. "He's slow" said the first-grade teacher who suggested I repeat that grade. Many years of struggle before I found ways to compensate for what was later determined to be a learning disability.

Over those years, I became overcompensating with the tenacity of a bulldog winning an award as the athlete "that did the most to make the varsity teams number one."

During my career that tenacity paid off and success seemed to flow to me and to my young family. That is until, during a budding sales position, my employers placed the challenge of advancement before me. After a successful sales year certainly, my employers would promote me. But no, they selected another person and again in the next year after a very successful year, they elected to promote two associates who had threatened to resign if not promoted. With all my best efforts and tenacious attitudes, I sat, humbled, at the national sales meeting, surrounded by my friends and close associates, as the promotion went to others.

After returning home with deep disappointment and even embarrassment at the repeated snub (to my thinking), I went to a men's prayer breakfast. At that breakfast, a church pastor asked about the sales meeting. Upon describing my experience, the pastor asked, "did you pray about this situation?" My response, "of course, I've never prayed for anything more than this". Then much to my surprise he exclaimed, "Alleluia, you got the answer to your prayer, you are blessed".

For my first thirty-eight years my belief was that all obstacles and challenges before me could simply be overcome by tenacity and hard work simply by my own will. The pastor had no idea how upset I was at his statement, but he profoundly changed my perspective about outcomes. From that day forward my life has been guided less by personal ambition and far more by a desire to be more family and community focused with a belief that much of our lives are not in our hands alone.

As a footnote, the next year, the employer did promote me only to see me move to another company. John H.

John loves the arts, frequenting museums, exhibits and art auctions. It led him to create paintings, stone carvings and sculptures, including several hundred castings of boxers' hands for the International Boxing Hall of Fame. He is a speaker, emcee and he has presided at Rotary, Stone Quarry Hill Art Park, Community Chest, Industrial Development Corp, and he found time to be a Scout leader for eighteen years.

Self-doubt

Most of my time is spent thinking — and that's not always a good thing.

True, it's usually best to consider what you're going to say *before* you say it. And if your thoughts are spiraling around an issue, that naturally lets you see it from several different perspectives. You're rarely blinded by certainty or confidence. But in my case, it often leaves me nervous: unsure of what I'm doing, who I am, or how I'm perceived.

I felt that most intensely when I started graduate school at the Newhouse School in Syracuse, NY. Everyone was a hustler, whip-smart and fast-moving. I started making mistakes — some real, some imagined — and the consequences of failure frightened me. Stress stopped giving me superpowers and just started to wear me out.

One of my classes was a review of the history and best practices of cultural critique. It required voicing and defending a fair number of my opinions. Despite my tendency to overanalyze, I love discussion. Several times I went out on a limb and embarrassed myself in that class.

Later in the semester, I had a one on one with my professor — a person I deeply admired — and, of course, I was nervous. It was becoming clear to me that I didn't have the drive to be a journalist, at least, not the way everyone else at Newhouse did. What would this professor think of me or my contributions to the class?

Our conversation was perhaps the most affirming I've ever had in my life. There are other people who have loved and supported me, but when they share their words of encouragement, it's like reinforcing a stout concrete overpass. It's appreciated, but I expected that structure to keep standing. (Hopefully without taking their words for granted.)

When my professor validated me, she was doing emergency repairs to a rickety wooden bridge. She said I was one of the most skilled students she'd had, that my insights were keen and my writing was clear. But I'll never forget that she told me I was a good person, that somehow, she could tell. I'm not sure if anyone who wasn't a close friend or family member has ever said that to me. For some reason, that meant more.

I continued to struggle at Newhouse, and even now, I haven't found more solid footing in a profession. But now when I'm filled with self-doubt or despair, I stop and remember my professor's words. I remind myself that even at my most stressed, someone saw the good in me. Even if I feel like it's not there, it's a north star I can aspire toward. It's a warmth in my heart when that warmth is sorely needed. Desmond G

The S. I. Newhouse School of Public Communications at Syracuse University, a top-rated program in the nation.

Accident

I had many experiences as an EMT and district supervisor with an ambulance company. It was also my privilege to teach school for a number of years. On my way to school one morning, I on-sited an accident where one of my students had been struck in a crosswalk by a car. Positioning my vehicle to block traffic, I moved to treat the injured student lying in the street. I told her she would be okay but that she should not try to move, and that help was on the way.

I continued to talk with her, explaining that I was keeping her spine stable while working my coat under her as protection from the really cold pavement. When the ambulance arrived, I helped get her loaded, leaving my coat under her. (My losing a coat when on-siting incidents while off-duty has become a bit of a joke around our house!) Next, I turned to the driver (another of my students) who also needed support and reassurance.

Years later, at a dance studio where my wife, Lou, was performing, I had an encounter I could never have anticipated. A familiar young woman by the cloak room turned suddenly and ran up to me, tearfully exclaiming, "My teacher! I was so frightened and so confused until you came, and then I knew I would be all right." She exuded poise and a confident manner that told me she was, indeed, "all right," even before we had a nice conversation where she caught me up on all she'd been doing since graduation. Although this story is primarily about how my words might have affected others, I must say that I was also affected by her words! Bob C

Commit

Years ago, I completed a 72-day Outward Bound course in California and Mexico. Outward Bound was originally founded to teach military personnel how to survive outdoors. Since then, it has evolved into an outdoor school for people around the world. Through each challenge with Outward Bound I learned significant lessons and struggled in the small group community we were forming. I believe that you often don't realize the lessons you are learning until later, when they play again in your head. One of the most poignant lessons has returned to me time and time again. Being "heavy-set" I am not a great rock climber. I'm also afraid of heights and have little upper body strength. In rock climbing you need to use your feet, but the tendency is to hold on tight with your arms and hands. This tires you out but feels the safest. To put weight on your feet you must trust your feet.

Joshua Tree National Monument is a desert filled with big piles of rocks. One day we were climbing, and I was at a point where the next hand hold was just out of reach. To keep going up, I needed to reach it. I carefully reached for it but couldn't make it. I searched for alternatives and tentatively kept re-trying for the hold out of reach. The instructor, after patiently waiting for me to explore all options, said "you have to **commit to the move**, you have to go for it with everything, without hesitancy." As I stood in my place of safety, his words sunk in. If I wanted to succeed, to make it to the top of the climb, I was at a place where I had to decide. Decide to trust, to commit, to move forward (up), or to throw in the towel and be lowered back to the ground. I only had one option, and I had to decide. Perched on the rock face, I went for it, with everything, I moved to the new foot hold, trusted my feet and

I committed, finishing the climb.

With each transition I have made, that lesson comes back. You can't change your life with hesitancy, you must '**commit to the move**'.

Excerpt from: *Launching Your Dreams: Making WILD Ideas Happen*, by Donna Lynn Price

Trust

In the process of thinking and writing about this experience, I realized that when one says something, speaking it out loud to another person, it becomes an actual entity, a "thing." It's no longer just a possibility, or a hope, or a wish, it's real. It's heard and recognized by both the speaker and the listener. And in the speaking and the hearing, the words become not only a reality, something solid, with boundaries-- but also a potential gift for both parties.

I worked for many years as a psychotherapist, spending time in conversations with clients--encouraging, sympathizing, empathizing, comforting, questioning, interpreting—all enacted through the use of words.

One afternoon I met with a client as part of ongoing psychotherapy. We had established and developed our relationship over many weeks, and enjoyed what I considered a positive, effective working relationship. On this particular day, the conversation flowed easily, with a feeling of ongoing connection. At one point, after a moment of quiet reflection, he looked at me directly and asked if I liked him.

I was surprised. I did like (as well as respect) him, appreciating the courage, strength, and honesty with which he tackled difficult issues. I was surprised because I had assumed that he knew that I liked him. I answered yes.

His question allowed us both to speak and connect more fully and deeply.   Clearly, he believed that deeper connection might be possible but didn't know for sure. Courageously, he used words to verify and solidify his feeling by asking me the question. His asking also gave me the opportunity to respond. Thus, his words transformed a feeling and question into a truth, something that he could trust and depend on.

From that time forward, we were able to work together more deeply, and on more difficult issues. Significantly, he appeared able to carry these skills into the future.   Lou C.

Deep & Dark Place

Some years ago, I was in a deep and dark place emotionally. I exhibited every crisis sign of suicide risk. I was abusing alcohol, prescription drugs, and withdrawing from family and friends, feeling hopeless, and looking for ways to kill myself. The emotional pain was far greater than any physical pain I ever experienced. Fortunately, my wife recognized my mental state and committed me to the acute psych ward at a local hospital for treatment and detox.

Upon discharge, I crawled into church the following Sunday. I don't remember much about the service as I spent much of the time just staring at the Cross above the sanctuary with tears in my eyes. The monotonous tone of the sermon did little to comfort me until I heard the words of St. Paul: "Do not be anxious about anything, but in every situation, by prayer and petition, with thanksgiving, present your requests to God."

"And the peace of God, which surpasses all understanding, will guard your hearts and minds in Christ Jesus" Philippians

4:6-7. I remembered the feeling of a significant burden being lifted off my shoulders and a profound sense of peace overwhelming me by those words that have been forever etched in my mind. I honestly was born again on that day.

This incarnational experience has taught me that we are all capable of overcoming our challenges and achieving greatness if we have faith and the strength that comes from the divine. It is a journey that requires dedication, reflection, and a willingness to embrace the power within us. And as I continue this path, I carry with me the profound realization that with faith, all things are possible.

To that end, today I work tirelessly with Veteran Service Organizations to educate both the public and veterans to recognize the signs of suicide risk to save lives. Veterans, particularly combat veterans, have a much higher suicide rate than the general public.

As a veteran myself and one who has travelled this road, it is my goal that my words and actions will result in saving one veteran's life from suicide.

Bill B.

Mythology

My son was probably about 8 years old when he asked me one day: "Do you have to be Christian to go to Heaven?" I remember the question so clearly, because while his inquisitiveness gave me pause, my response was immediate and heartfelt, rooted in a "lesson" I had learned more than a decade earlier from a very wise college professor.

While historically affiliated with the Lutheran Church, my college was nonsectarian in that it welcomed students and faculty of all or no faith traditions. I had grown up in the Christian church, always faithfully attending Sunday school and worship services with my parents, singing in the junior and senior choirs, and participating in youth group activities throughout my childhood and youth. At college, I very quickly felt at home among other openly professing Christian students. It's not that I thought deeply about what it meant to be a Christian or to embrace the tenets of the Christian tradition; it was just that Christianity was all I had ever known. I came from a small, heavily white, Protestant town in south central Pennsylvania, where I knew exactly one Jewish student in my entire high school. There may have been some from other faith traditions, but if there were, I didn't know them.

In my sophomore year of college, I enrolled in a class titled "Religion and Mythology," and while I'm not sure what I had expected from it, I was appalled when in those early classes, my professor made reference to what he called the "Jesus myth." I was indignant. How DARE he question the foundational figure of my faith! What kind of religion professor was he anyway? After a few classes, I decided to confront him on it during his office hours.

As soon as I sat down in his office, I blurted out all of my indignation (with perhaps a touch of self-righteousness). "How can you, as a professor of *religion*, talk about Christianity as a myth? What kind of lesson is that for your students? Aren't you a Christian?"

To his credit, my professor listened patiently until I had finished. Then he said, simply, that yes, while he is a religion professor, it is not his job to produce converts to the faith. His job was to teach students about religious traditions and, in this particular course, the connections between the historical roots of those traditions and the making of myths, which he believes are themselves rooted in truth.

It was simple enough. He could have stopped there. He had gently exposed my naivete in conflating the study of religion in a college classroom with becoming "religious." But he didn't stop. He went on to answer my inappropriately challenging question by saying that, yes, in fact, he *was* a practicing Christian and that he attended the local Mennonite church down the road. He paused a moment and then added that while he called himself a Christian, he did not believe that Christianity was the only way to live a God-filled life.

"Jesus tells us in John 14:2 that 'In my Father's house are many rooms,'" he said. "I believe that means there is a place for believers of all faiths—and that when I die and go to Heaven, I will see my Jewish friends there, and my Hindu friends there, and my Muslim friends all there in God's kingdom of many rooms."

I can't recall my immediate reaction other than that I felt mollified and maybe a bit sheepish. But his words would have a profound effect on me. They prompted me to take a closer look at my own belief system in a way I never had prior. A few years later, now as a young adult, I decided to switch churches after a Sunday school class of my peers took me to task for not trying to convert a Jewish workplace colleague to Christianity. They saw that as a sin. With the words of my former professor ringing in my ears—that there are many pathways to God—I saw their condemnation as a sign this class, this particular church, was a bad fit for me.

A decade later, the words came flooding back as I listened to my son question whether Heaven was reserved solely for Christians. I shared with him the same message my very wise, very compassionate, professor had shared with me—words that reshaped my personal spiritual trajectory, deepening my faith even as it expanded my belief in an all-inclusive, all-loving God for all people.

A few years ago, when I got word of my former professor's planned retirement, I wrote him a note to tell him about the transformative effect that conversation had had on me as an individual and, later, as a parent. And I thanked him for taking the time to share with me in a way that, while perhaps falling outside his formal purview as a "professor of religion," had a more profound impact on me than any classroom lesson I can recall to this day. Carol B

Weeping Woman

My retirement job is captaining a passenger ferry off the coast of Connecticut. I take residents to a group of 26 islands called the Thimbles. Most days I agree with passengers who comment "you have the best office in the world."

One mid-summer afternoon I was waiting for my next trip in a shady gazebo on the dock. My mindless phone scrolling was interrupted by the sound of muted sobbing coming from a solitary figure, a woman, seated on the seawall 20 yards away. Was she OK? Had she hurt herself? Had someone hurt her? Should I check on her? Should I mind my own business?

After a few minutes as the sobbing continued, I approached her and inquired if she was Ok? Here is her story:

She had just come from Smilow Cancer Center in New Haven with a diagnosis that every woman fears. On her way home she had driven down to the dock to be with the only person in her life she felt safe enough to share the jarring news... her father. She had scattered his ashes in the water close to that very spot several years ago.

I sat there as she gradually unfolded her health journey and her newly reinforced fears. What does a 70-year-old retired guy have to say? Not much. So, I listened.

My next ferry run was scheduled to leave the dock. "I tell you what" I said. "I'm wondering if a ride on the ferry could let the breeze blow out some of that anxiety. Come on, the ride is on me".

I don't remember much after that. She stood towards the bow and as I looked out of the pilot house, she seemed to let her head catch the wind. She thanked me as she got off the boat and disappeared in the parking lot. I hoped she was going to be okay but soon forgot our encounter.

…Until I received a card in the mail over a year later. It was addressed to the ferry company with my name. "I don't know if you remember me. You gave me a ride on the ferry when I'd just come back from Smilow and had stopped on the shoreline to be with my "Dad." She reported on her life since then. She'd repaired and sold her house nearby and bought another further away. She'd been in and out of hospital appointments and had surgery. She hoped that "all the cells were out". What followed was a thank you for the ferry ride that day. "I know without a doubt, my Dad orchestrated me meeting you because that ferry ride was exactly what I needed. I'm including my New's Years card, and as you can see there is no mention of my health issue. You are one of three people who know." Jeff W.

Personal Reflection & Notes:

SEVEN

OTHER CHANGE STORIES

A New Media Voice

An idea was born. Pamila Illott, the first female vice president of CBS Television, suggested a program idea to Harry C. Spencer, top executive of the Methodist Church's Television, Radio and Film Commission.

Night Call was the first national call-in show in the nation. It was designed to bring a national audience into dialogue around major faith, moral and ethical issues facing our society. It was rolled out in test markets across the country with Russ Gibbs, a Michigan radio personality, as host. Producer was Rev.

Stanley Knock. The format was host in studio, guest on telephone line, and audience callers. The limitations of the technology were immediately apparent. It was a nightmare – squawk, crackle, pop – "can you hear me now, are you still there?" We pulled the program off the air and went to an audio inventor/genius, Warren Braun, to design equipment. It took nearly a year. The result was a console slightly smaller than a spinet piano.

In the meantime, Martin Luther King, Jr., was assassinated. The country was a tinder box. Cities were burning. Rioters were raiding retail stores. Violence was rampant. Death lurked around many corners. We turned the corner from its original purpose to creating dialogue with the nation's radio audience about what was happening across the country.

We thought *Night Call* might serve as a place of dialogue and healing. Leaders of all stripes – angry Black African leaders like Stokely Carmichael and Rap Brown, politicians like presidential candidate Hubert Humphrey, and religious leaders like the Rev. Ralph Abernathy, successor to Martin Luther King, Jr. There were national leaders in journalism, psychology, sociology and more. After a brief interview with the guest, members of the radio audience called in to ask the guest a question.

Guests rarely refused to appear. Movement leaders could be guests even when they were hiding from the FBI. Norman Cousins, prominent journalist and author, called after he landed at an airport. We hoped the dialogue would help diffuse anger and violence.

With a new purpose we needed a Black host. Through church connections, we found Del Shields, a jazz disc jockey on

Harlem's WLIB radio station, the son of a black bishop of a church in Brooklyn. (Shields later attended seminary and became a pastor in New York City).

We broadcasted from the WRVR studios, a jazz station, in Riverside Church in New York City.

When the equipment was ready to be installed, the telephone company installer took a look at the box and said, "I've got to check with the office. I can't connect it." We were days from launch, and the publicity had already gone out.

I soon had a call from New York Bell that they couldn't allow us to connect our equipment – the number of incoming calls would run the risk of "crashing the system."

Our producer, Ben Logan, had created an Advisory Committee of prominent professionals. Two were members of Congress. Ben called each Congressman. A day later, I received a call from the president of NY Bell. He said, "I don't know what's going on, but Washington says to put you guys on the air. What we're going to do," he said, "is put you on the Wall Street exchange. It's completely dark at night." In 1968, Wall Street was only a financial and business center. It was much later that it became residential. *Night Call* launched in June 1968.

New York Bell was right. On the heaviest nights, as many as 41,000 attempts were made to reach the show. Some were repeat callers, but it represented a significant audience of an estimated 4,000,000. At the peak, there were 119 stations, from 50,000-watt clear channel stations to 5000-watt small town stations. We blanketed the country allowing rich and poor, rural and urban, naïve and sophisticated people to talk with guests while the audience listened in. Then, they were invited to participate.

Night Call aired from 11:30 p.m. to 12:30 a.m. in the eastern time zone and started at 8:30 p.m. in the west, five nights a week. It aired live and blanketed the country. At that time, only local disc jockeys, local talk shows and syndicated packaged programs were on the air. Night was not valuable commercial time. And radio stations had an obligation to fulfill FCC (Federal Communications Commission) requirements to carry public service programming. But they also saw what was happening in their communities and across the nation. They wanted to be part of the solution.

The Ford Foundation recognized the possibilities of *Night Call* by contributing $400,000, a huge amount in the 60's ($4,000,000 in 2025 dollars). The Methodist Church gave substantial financial support and others more modest sums.

While produced by The United Methodist Church's Television, Radio and Film Commission (TRAFCO), it was sponsored by the National Council of Churches, the U.S. Catholic Office for Radio and Television, and the National Urban League. It received fantastic press from most of the mainline media as well as Variety and Broadcasting Magazine, plus many awards. It reflected well on the stations which carried it.

It ran for 19 months. Ultimately, the cost could not be sustained. Contributions were the only sources of income. Advertisers were afraid of the controversy.

There was symbolic power in *Night Call*. It showed how the religious community came together in the belief that dialogue could help heal our wounds, that if aggrieved persons could feel they were being heard, violence might be avoided. Perhaps

Night Call could play a moderating role during a national crisis.

By the end of airing, towns and cities had calmed down. Life was more normal.

Did Night Call change lives, calm the night, bring new insights and beliefs? Were some listeners so affected that a new belief was incarnated into their souls so deeply that it changed the direction of their lives?

What we know is that media can change behavior, i.e., why advertise? We also now know that talk radio can have strong negative effects on their listeners through disinformation, conspiracy theories, and misinformation. Listeners can be influenced to think that our "government is a swamp," every politician is dishonest, that white people will soon be the minority and discriminated against, losing power.

Talk radio can reinforce biases of the many "isms —sexism, racism, ageism, ableism, heterosexism (i.e., homophobia), classism, sizeism, and antisemitism. Our biases can be conscious or unconscious. They have real world consequences. They reinforce oppression and inequities in our culture.

A Life Changed

 The Odyssey Cable Network was launched in 1987 as an alternative to the many televangelists who were getting rich from subscribers of cable systems. It was a coalition of 67 denominations and faith communities – Protestant, Catholic and Jewish, from conservative to liberal and most in-between. There were three basic principles: No on-air fund-raising; no proselytizing of another faith; no attacking of another faith group. Simply present your faith as strongly and persuasively as you can.

The network's mission statement was "Making Faith Visible on Television." Programming was varied; a significant number were provided by member faith groups; some were acquired from other producers, and many were produced by the network.

One of the popular programs was *Common Sense Religion* on Sunday evenings when Dr. Gerald Mann, a prominent Austin, Texas, pastor, took questions from callers about faith and personal belief.

One night, a call came from a woman in a Western state. She was obviously dealing with a deep emotional issue, and Dr. Mann recognized it as too serious for public discussion. He asked her to leave her number with the producer and promised to call her back after the show.

He called on his way home. She answered, but he could tell from the slowness and slurring of her speech and some incoherence, that she might have taken pills to end her life. He hung up and called 911 in her area code and said, "I think there may be an attempted suicide at this number." Emergency medics reached her home in time to save her life.

Two or three weeks later, Dr. Mann received another call from the woman. She was outraged. How dare he interfere in her personal life! Dr. Mann explained that as a Christian pastor, and because she had called him, there was no alternative for him but to intervene. She hung up in anger!

A year later, Dr. Mann heard from her again. This time she thanked him for saving her life. She had reconciled with her children. She had a new job. Life was good!

Remember psychiatrist Berne's observation. "One never knows when a word or a phrase may change someone's life." Every one of us is a change agent!

John Wesley and Slavery

Not all change is an incarnational moment. Change also comes gradually step by step. Look at who you were in your 20's, and who you are now. Have your beliefs and priorities changed?

Changed happened slowly for John Newton, a Christian and a slave ship captain. Owning enslaved people was a part of the culture. Newton thought captaining slave ships was his calling as a Christian. He captained three slave ships. On the last, he became seriously ill. He quit as captain but continued to invest in slave trading.

Newton had several jobs before deciding to enter seminary. John Wesley invited him to join the Methodist movement, but he chose the Church of England. He pastored several churches and was a popular preacher. Newton is the writer of the popular hymn, *Amazing Grace.*

The movement to abolish slavery in England was growing.

At that time, pamphleteering was the mass medium and an effective way to reach the public. Wesley was a strong, unbending opponent of slavery. He spent the last third of his life opposing and working for the abolition of slavery and wrote widely distributed pamphlets against slavery.

Newton slowly moved to oppose slavery. He testified against slavery before Parliament and became a strong abolitionist. It was asked if Wesley was the primary factor in opposing slavery. The answer was no, but a major factor.

The abolition of slavery in England changed North America. Canada was a part of the British Empire, so slavery also was illegal there. It created a second safe haven for escaped slaves, the Mexican Border and all along the Northern Border but especially from Detroit east to the Atlantic Ocean. Niagara Falls was a major crossing at a narrow place in the Niagara River. Slaves descended over 500 steps to be taken across in a rowboat.

The abolitionist crusade by John Wesley in England created a safe refuge in Canada for U.S. slaves as well as crossing the border of Mexico. For the first time, slaves had two land boundaries they could cross to freedom. It changed the lives of millions of human beings.

Nelson Mandela

South Africa for centuries had an all-white colonial government in a predominantly black country. The Dutch arrived in 1652 and found a land rich in resources. It was worth fighting for and there were many players.

In modern times, the government establish apartheid, a system which marginalized the blacks and favored the whites. Nelson Mandella was the Black leader of the opposition to the all-white South African government, campaigning to overthrow it. Mandella was such a threat that he was imprisoned and in solitary confinement for most of 27 years.

During that time, Catholic and Protestant religious groups brought pressure on U.S. companies to dis-invest in South Africa until reform was undertaken. It influenced the economy. Racial tensions increased.

Under fear of racial war, the president released Mandela in

1990. I'm sure many expected Mandela to come out a broken and bitter man. He came out strong and still energized. He became president in May 1994 and served until June 1999.

Mandela loved his country so much that he chose reconciliation instead of retribution. His people had been abused, tortured, jailed, murdered. Yet, he established the Truth and Reconciliation Commission (TRC). Wikipedia chronicled the commission's work:

> *The Truth and Reconciliation Commission (TRC) was a court-like restorative justice body assembled in South Africa in 1996 after the end of apartheid. Authorised by Nelson Mandela and chaired by Desmond Tutu, the commission invited witnesses who were identified as victims of gross human rights violations to give statements about their experiences, and selected some for public hearings. Perpetrators of violence could also give testimony and request amnesty from both civil and criminal prosecution.*

> *The mandate of the commission was to bear witness to, record, and in some cases grant amnesty to the perpetrators of crimes relating to human rights violations, as well as offering reparation and rehabilitation to the victims. A register of reconciliation was also established so that ordinary South Africans who wished to express regret for past failures could also express their remorse.*

> *The TRC had a number of high-profile members, including Archbishop Desmond Tutu (chairman), Alex Boraine (deputy chairman), Sisi Khampepe, Wynand Malan, Klaas de Jonge and Emma Mashinini.*

Mandela is an example of a non-violent solution to a conflict situation.

Mandela expressed interest in visiting the United States. When Jeff Weber and Bruno Caliandro, the creative team at the fledgling VISN cable network, later named Odyssey, proposed we invite Mandela to speak at a NYC church, I was skeptical. Would it simply be a time-consuming rabbit hole?

They said, "He should not come to the U.S. without speaking to the religious community which worked so hard and long for his release." It was an audacious move. It seemed improbable Mandela would accept. In addition, the network had no money to produce a live two-hour television special.

VISN/Odyssey launched October 1, 1988. It was a coalition of denominations and faith communities in partnership with Telecommunications, Inc., the largest cable operator in the country. The Rev. Daniel Mathews, rector of Trinity Episcopal Church located on Wall Street in New York City, was president of the Board. I was president/CEO of the network, Jeff Weber, talented producer, was Vice President, and the Rev. Bruno Caliandro, an experienced network television producer and consultant, was Creative Director.

Caliandro approached the Rev. James Forbes, senior minister of the famous Riverside Church on New York's upper Westside. He immediately accepted. They invited Mandela to make the Riverside Church his first major stop in the U.S.A. A reply came almost immediately. He would be delighted.

When Bishops and pastors of African American churches in the city learned of the invitation, they thought Mandela should speak in a traditional Black Church. Forbes was Black. The congregation had a large Black membership, but traditionally, was White.

We stewed over what we should do for two or three days. Then we had a *brilliant idea*. Why not ask Mandela what he preferred?

The answer came back quickly. Mandela wanted to speak from the pulpit where The Rev. Martin Luther King, Jr., had delivered his sermon opposing the Vietnam war in 1966. The date was set: June 21, 1990, at 12 noon.

Now the planning moved into action. Caliandro contacted his friend at Madison Square Garden, Frank O'Connell, head of the Garden's remote television unit. It primarily covered sports and outdoor events. The control room and video equipment were carried in a huge semi-truck trailer. It was parked on Riverside Drive next to the church. Grant's Tomb was across the street.

The costs were projected at $65,000 (2025 value $158,000). A corporate fund-raiser, Jack DuVall, presented the project to several New York companies. Time was short, but it turned out to be an advantage. NYNEX and Colgate-Palmolive Company stepped forward. Smaller funders included the Black Programming Consortium and the Reformed Church in America. The funding was secured!

We later learned that the wife of the president of Colgate-Palmolive was a longtime supporter of Mandela and his cause. NYNEX wanted to demonstrate to its employees their commitment to black issues.

Security

Normally when a public official comes to the United States, their protection team coordinates the safety of their leader with the U.S. Secret Service. Mandela was a private citizen. He had no security team.

The U.S. wanted nothing to happen to Mandela while in the United States. All staff members, crews, and choir had to be cleared by the Secret Service. Secret Service agents were in the

2,400-seat sanctuary and in the two large overflow rooms, where 1,000 attendees were watching TV screens. Hundreds of New Yorkers gathered outside the church on that warm, June, day, hoping to catch a glimpse of Mandela, now a world hero, a representative of courage, endurance and freedom.

As I walked outside, I looked down Riverside Drive. There were sharp shooters on the roofs of apartment buildings lining the Avenue. I think I spotted one in the tower of the church.

There were five police jurisdictions involved and to be coordinated. The Secret Service. The New York City Police. The Sherriff's Department. The Park Service, because the event was across the street from Grant's Tomb. In addition, the State Police accompanied the motorcade across the city to the church.

After the service, a woman in one of the viewing rooms started to leave to get ahead of the crowd. A Secret Service agent told her to sit back down. No one was moving before Mandela was out of the building.

I was outside after the service. The crowd was dense. Whenever someone started to move from their position, a Secret Service agent required them to stay put. No one was moving until Mandela was out of the building.

The Worship and Celebration Service

Forbes and Caliandro planned a service that would flow for television and work for those in the sanctuary. A robed floor director sat with choir, cueing speakers to the pulpit or the lectern. There were seven cameras in the sanctuary. Caliandro directed. The on-camera hosts were Bill Turpie, a VISN regular, and Leslie Crosson, a TV personality.

The heads of all faith groups in New York City -- Protestant, Catholic, Greek Orthodox, Jewish and Muslim – participated. Political leaders were invited. The choir was a combination of members from Riverside and Harlem churches. It was an ecumenical and interfaith event.

When clergy and dignitaries were lined up to enter the sanctuary, Caliandro said, "Cue the processional!" Then quickly, "Start the processional!" A group of African drummers led, moving down the long center aisle. Winnie and Nelson Mandela followed. Then came three Secret Service agents, scanning the filled sanctuary. The congregation rose to its feet, cheering and applauding. The atmosphere was electric and celebratory.

Pastor James Forbes and New York City Mayor David N. Dinkins eloquently welcomed the Mandelas. Jesse Jackson, prominent civil rights champion and a future candidate for president, gave the opening prayer.

The music by the choir and soloists was inspiring.

The congregation was brought to its feet, applauding and cheering, when Dr. Gardner Taylor, prominent Harlem minster, said, "I present the true leader of South Africa, certified by his own courage and integrity, ratified by the blood of countless South Africans, confirmed by people of decency everywhere. I present to you the moral lead of the world, the stand bearers of freedom, the drum major in the music of freedom." The congregation stood again and applauded for several minutes until Mandela, now in the pulpit, appealed for quiet.

Mandela spoke. "During our long years in prison, you did not forget us. You took up the mission of promoting justice and peace. We salute you. We thank you. It is a precious gift."

The service was two hours long, but the 35 Public TV stations stayed with us, sharing the event with their audiences and school children. The three major television networks were caught flat footed, not realizing the significance of the event until it was too late to participate. CBS had one camera in the sanctuary. The Madison Square Garden crew had seven. Each of the major networks relied on this new, fledgling cable network for its evening news footage! It was a small victory in the media world.

The bigger impact was much more significant. Disparate religious and political groups came together to honor a growing world figure. It reminded the nation of the egregious injustices of apartheid and lifted up the role the religious community had in bringing it to an end. It honored the integrity and resilience of a heroic leader. And it proposed that we might all have the capability of heroic acts in our own relationships. Hopefully, it planted seeds for justice and fairness and equality, recognizing how one individual can make a huge difference, if not globally, perhaps in our own communities and families.

Personal Reflection & Notes:

EIGHT

LOVE

The most powerful *words* in the world -- regardless of faith, race, ethnicity, sexual orientation, country, or language – are, **"I LOVE YOU."**

As a change agent, Love is your most powerful force.

Why is it, then, so hard to say, "I love you?" Is it because we fear being rejected? Or misunderstood? Too audacious? Too uncommon? Maybe flirting? Really weird?

I have a friend who reports his father never told him he loved him. He knows he did, but he never said it.

When our family of forty or so tell each other we love them, it changes the dynamics of the family; it binds us together. It helps each to know we care about them and care about how they are doing, regardless of their sexual identity, political or religious beliefs. It has become easy and not perfunctory.

When a refugee friend, who had to leave his family or go to prison for his political activities, told me he loved me, it changed me and changed our relationship. It brought us closer together and deepened our relationship. It created a greater sense of concern for him and sense of responsibility for his welfare.

When I became freer to tell my friends "I love you." The response usually was, "I love you, too." It always changed our relationship for the better. The power of love – and being loved.

Much has been written throughout the ages about *love*. I write simply as a reminder and an affirmation of what you already know and have experienced.

All the great faiths: Christian, Muslim, Jewish, Buddhist, Hindu, have recognized *Love* as a powerful force – a common belief and reality that can unify us as one human race. Christian author Ruth Haley Barton, wrote, "Love is the deepest calling of the Christian life, the standard by which everything about our lives is measured. Any decision-making process that fails to ask the love question misses the point of the Christian practice of discernment." [14]

In the Christian Bible, recorded in Mark 12:30-31, Jesus was asked by a teacher of the law, "Of all the commandments, which is the most important?" Jesus answered, "Love the Lord

---

[14] Ruth Haley Barton , "Listening for the Divine Voice: Weekly Summary, Center for Action and Contemplation. October 26, 2024, https://cac.org/daily-meditations/listening-for-the-divine-voice-weekly-summary.

your God with all your heart and with all your soul and with all your mind and with all your strength. The second is this: Love your neighbor as yourself. There is no commandment greater than these." Jesus even went further. In Matthew 5:44 (NIV), Jesus instructs and challenges his followers to "love your enemies and pray for those who persecute you."

The Rev. Dr. Martin Luther King, Jr. believed in the power of love to change the hearts and minds of "those who persecute you." He said in a Christmas sermon on peace:

We shall match your capacity to inflict suffering by our capacity to endure suffering. We will meet your physical force with soul force. Do to us what you will and we will still love you. We cannot in all good conscience obey your unjust laws and abide by the unjust system, because noncooperation with evil is as much a moral obligation as is cooperation with good and so throw us in jail and we will still love you. Bomb our homes and threaten our children, and, as difficult as it is, we will still love you.… But be assured that we'll wear you down by our capacity to suffer, and one day we will win our freedom. We will not only win freedom for ourselves, we will so appeal to your heart and conscience that we will win you in the process, and our victory will be a double victory."[15]

In writing about the power of non-violence, Richard Deats, of the Fellowship of Reconciliation, wrote that non-violence, "is truth force, love force in action."

John Love, a Catholic priest and peace advocate, said there were three requirements for love in action: "love yourself, love

---

[15] Richard Deats, *Martin Luther King, Jr. Spirit-Led Prophet,* New City Press, 2000, pg. 125.

others, move into action in the community." [16]

The Rev. James M. Lawson, Jr., who was a United Methodist pastor, teacher of non-violence and an activist in the Civil Rights Movement, said, "Love is power. It is the most creative power in the universe. It is the greatest force that is available to humankind. Humankind needs to learn how to use it." [17]

John Wesley, the founder of the Methodist movement (1703-1791), said, "Though we cannot think alike, may we not love alike? May we not be of one heart, though we are not of one opinion?"[18]

The Apostle Paul placed love above all other beliefs and values, even before faith. In First Corinthians 13:13, Paul wrote, "And now these three remain: faith, hope and love. But *the greatest of these is love.*"

The forces of power, greed and oppression are still rampant, threatening democracies, care for our planet, care for all human life, and so much more.

Every generation, every family, every individual face their own challenges. That is why it's so important for everyone to recognize their powers to create change, in themselves and in others. While *Change Agent* is not therapy because there is no

---

[16] Fr. John Love, Lecture at St. Lucy's Roman Catholic Church, Syracuse, N.Y., April 18, 2024.

[17] Anthony Siracusa, "Civil Rights Leader James Lawson, Who Learned from Gandhi, Used Nonviolent Resistance and the 'Power of Love' To Challenge Injustice." The Conversation, June 13, 2024. https://theconversation.com/civil-rights-leader-james-lawson-who-learned-from-gandhi-used-nonviolent-resistance-and-the-power-of-love-to-challenge-injustice-232232.

[18] General Commission on Archives and History, "John Wesley Speaks on Love," The United Methodist Church, 2025, https://www.umc.org/-/media/umc-media/2024/04/08/20/41/John%20Wesley%20on%20Love.pdf

professional therapist guiding the conversation, it may be therapeutic. It may help you have your own Aha, incarnational experience.

Addressing a world faced with consumerism, division and artificial intelligence, Pope Francis urged the faithful in 2024 to "return to the heart: In a word, if love reigns in our heart, we become, in a complete and luminous way, the persons we are meant to be, for every human being is created above all else for love. In the deepest fiber of our being, we were made to love and to be loved." [19]

Episcopal Bishop Michael Curry has written, "The way of love will show us the right thing to do, every single time. It is moral and spiritual grounding—and a place of rest—amid the chaos that is often part of life. It's how we stay decent in indecent times." [20]

Jesus also spoke of the power of faith. In the Parable of the Mustard Seed, recorded in Matthew 13, Mark 4 and Luke 13, Jesus said, "if we have even the faith of the small mustard seed, we can move mountains."

Bottom line: Love is more powerful than faith. Love can move mountains. I believe the "mountains" we can and need to "move" through love are the mountains of hate, prejudice, sexism, racism, homophobia, militarism, violence, and all mountains which divide us. We do this starting in our own homes, workplaces, schools – with our children, our families,

[19] Jorge Mario Bergoglio, "Encyclical Letter of the Holy Father Francis on The Human and Divine Love of the Heart of Jesus Christ," The Holy See, October 24, 2024, https://www.vatican.va/content/francesco/en/encyclicals/documents/20241024-enciclica-dilexit-nos.html.
[20] Michael Curry, *"Love Takes Commitment,"* Center for Contemplation and Action, November 7, 2024, https://cac.org/daily-meditations/love-takes-commitment .

our friends -- everywhere we are – through our words and actions.

In the God's Word translation of Acts 10:34-35 Peter said, "Now I understand that God doesn't play favorites. Rather, whoever respects God and does what is right is acceptable to him in any nation." Most translations use "whoever fears God…is acceptable…" But some Biblical scholars suggest a more accurate translation is respect. "Whoever *respects* God…is acceptable." [21]

Persons who come to faith through fear may be loyal followers – but not true believers. We do not love another because of our fears. We do not avoid "hell" because we fear God. We do good because we are loved unconditionally by God.

While I have referenced Christian and Jewish affirmations of the power of love, all of the great faith traditions speak about love, and challenge every human being to be better.

Buddhism:

Real love means loving-kindness and compassion, the kind of love that does not have any conditions. You form a community of two in order to practice love—taking care of each other, helping your partner blossom, and making happiness something real in that small community. Through your love for each other, through learning the art of making one person happy, you learn to express your love for the whole of humanity and all beings.[22]

---

[21]Acts 10:34, God's Word Translation, Bible Gateway, Accessed April 25, 2025, https://www.biblegateway.com/passage/?search=Acts%2010%3A34-43&version=GW;NIV

[22] Thich Naht Hanh, *Your True Home: The Everyday Wisdom,* (Shambala Publications Inc., 2011), page 330.

Hindu:

Love is not just an emotion, it's our very existence, it's woven through all of creation. And the more we see it and the more we experience this, it allows our life to become an expression of that love. [23]

By whatever name *you* call the forces of creation and the forces for good, I call that force, God. I believe we are doing the will of God – the will of the universe, when we create beauty, do useful work, love those we encounter, become better human beings. We move closer to the vision of MLK, Jr., "the beloved community." [24]

When LOVE is incarnate in our souls and our psyches – love flows into our relationships and community.

In the end, LOVE is our only hope. Every action, every word, should be prefaced with,

"DO I DO THIS IN LOVE?"

I know what was said – I don't know what was heard.

I hope the case has been made -- a paradigm shift of our understanding in the power of our words and how our words can be "incarnational," transformational. They can change lives. You are a Change Agent. You are blessed with great power.

---

[23] Juliette Plummer, "The Transformational Power of Love in Hinduism," John Templeton Foundation, June 21, 2023, https://www.templeton.org/news/the-transformational-power-of-love-in-hinduism .
[24] Martin Luther King, Jr. Center for Nonviolent Social Change, *"The King Philosophy – Nonviolence 365,"* The King Center, accessed April 29, 2025, https://thekingcenter.org/about-tkc/the-king-philosophy/

Personal Reflection & Notes:

NINE

SYSTEMIC CHANGE

Television – A Change Agent

A brief overview: In the 1950's, television was a new medium. It had been delayed for public use by World War II. The decade saw a dramatic rise in advertising, entertainment and news. By 1955, half the homes in the U.S. had black and white television sets. By 1959, the figure was 86 percent. It was a social and cultural revolution!

There were four national networks: Columbia Broadcasting System (CBS), National Broadcasting Network (NBC), the American Broadcasting Network (ABC), and the Westinghouse Broadcasting Network (WBN). They dominated the media scene.

Television was established as a commercial enterprise to make money unlike utilities of electricity and water. Its primary mission is to gather viewers to sell to advertisers. The advertising revenue supports all programming. Shows that do not attract an audience are dropped.

In the beginning, the Federal Communications Commission (FCC) required stations to serve in "the public interest" and to provide local groups opportunities to provide "public service" programming. They were required to balance their programming with various viewpoints (The Fairness Doctrine). And to serve their local communities.

At first, many TV stations were locally, and family-owned. They were part of the community. As FCC leadership changed, ownership rules were changed so that more and more stations could be owned by one company, thus concentrating the influence of larger and larger media companies.

In the 1960's, there was a growing interest in the impact of televised violence on values, beliefs, attitudes and behavior of viewers. Especially, what was its effect on children? Since one of the ways children learn is by watching and imitating behavior by those around them, it was reasonable to conclude that television could teach both good and bad behavior or even have no effect. Early research was controversial.

In 1971, the U.S. Surgeon General issued a report on the findings of 69 research studies by university behavioral scientists on the effects of televised violence on children and adults. Sixty-eight found harmful effects.

Dr. Eli A. Rubinstein, vice chair of the Surgeon General's Scientific Advisory Committee and co-editor of the reports, concluded:

While there is indeed no scientific evidence that excessive viewing of televised violence can or does provoke violent crime in any one individual, it is clear that the bulk of the studies show that if large groups of children watch a great deal of televised violence they will be more prone to behave aggressively than similar groups of children who do not watch such TV violence. The argument simply follows from the basic premise that children learn from all aspect of their environment. [25]

Adults also are affected by the amount of television they watch, especially detective and crime programs. Larry Gross, at the time a communication professor at the University of Pennsylvania, reported on a poll that *The Morning Herald* of Hagerstown, Maryland, conducted of city residents. It showed that "almost two-thirds of the people polled fear for their safety after dark—despite the fact that they know that crime rates (in Hagerstown) are relatively low…heavy TV viewers…tended to overestimate all the crime figures they were asked to offer opinions on…"[26]

In another study of children and adult viewers, "In case after case, heavy viewers of television are more likely than are light viewers to answer questions about the real world in terms which seem to reflect the facts of life in the symbolic world of television drama." [27]

The belief that the symbolic television world is the real world has real life consequences. Heavy viewers go into the city less,

[25] Ben Logan, editor, *Television Awareness Training*, (Abingdon Press, 1979), page 64.
[26] Logan, page 21.
[27] Logan, page 21.

affecting the urban economy. They are more fearful. They spur the gun economy. Unsecured guns in the home kill children and adults.

Children fear the dark. They are more aggressive with other children. Heavy child viewers think it's alright to hit someone. They see who is important and powerful (men), and who is weak and needs help (women). Gross also wrote that "Television provides the broadest common background of assumptions about what things are, how they work (or should work), and why." [28] While the research is dated, human nature has not changed. I think the research is still relevant today.

Here are several steps you can take to secure your agency or control over your and your families' television experiences. (From Television Awareness Training curriculum)

1. Don't leave the TV on all day. Be selective in what you watch.
2. Be selective in what your children watch.
3. When watching with children and a scary moment arrives, ask "how do you think they did that?", bringing them the realization that the show was "made" by someone, it's not necessarily real.
4. Ask the question, "How much is television using me, and how much am I using TV?"
5. Discuss programs: violence, how problems are solved, the values proposed and how they differ from your values. Who has the power? Who are victims? How are women, minorities, people of

---

[28] Logan, page 21.

color or persons of different sexual orientation portrayed? Positively, negatively?

As staff members of communications agencies of major denominations, we thought it imperative that we understand the effects of television so we could help equip the millions of families in our congregations to deal with those negative effects in a positive way.

Television Awareness Training (TAT)

TAT was a project of the Media Action Research Center (MARC), a consortium of Protestant and Catholic communications executives. It was headquartered in United Methodist Communications offices in New York City. Officers and staff were: Nelson Price, president; Ben Logan, program director; Shirley Struchen, executive director; Dr. Robert M. Liebert, scientific director and a research professor at the State University of New York at Stoney Brook, Long Island; Stanley Nelson and Jeff Weber, staff.

MARC created a workshop curriculum to train leaders and educators on how to mitigate harmful effects of television. The curriculum included "clips" from TV network programs illustrating TV's potentially harmful effects. A 270-page book was published of articles and work exercises by national researchers. It was edited by Ben Logan. Workshops were held across the country and in several foreign countries to train leaders. Hundreds were trained.

It was early in the "Media Literacy Movement." The faith community with its millions of adherents energized the movement. MARC established a laboratory on Long Island to test how positive messages in a 30-second TV spot might change a child's behavior when faced with violent acts of pushing, shoving, hitting, to positive alternative ways to resolve those conflict situations.

Surprisingly, the spots were effective. As a result, Dr. Liebert and I testified before the Communications Committees of both the House and the Senate. With the provision of free speech in the constitution, it was not possible to create legislation to control violence on television.

In a meeting with top CBS executives, the director of research told me that if they believed what I was telling them, they'd have to change most of their children's programming." Cartoons were especially violent.

Two outstanding programs on Public Broadcasting System (PBS) television demonstrated the positive effects television programming could have on children: Sesame Street and Mr. Roger's Neighborhood. When TV executives acknowledged how TV could have a positive influence on children, they also had to recognize its negative effects too. Couldn't have one without the other.

Denominations and communication executives that participated in creating TAT were: American Lutheran Church, Harry Souders; Christian Church (Disciples of Christ), Rev. Fred Erickson; Reformed Church in America, Rev. Peter Paulsen; United Church of Christ, Ralph Jennings; Church of the Brethren, Stewart Hoover; Presbyterian Church in the U.S., Betty Miller McMaster; Protestant Episcopal Church, Sonia Francis; United Methodist Church, Nelson Price, Ben Logan, Shirley Struchen; World Association for Christian Communication (WACC), Thelma Awori; United Church of Canada, Keith Woollard.

Television and the Economy

Television's impact was not simply on the messages it delivers and the audiences it gathers. *It changed the structure of the economy* in the U.S.

Canadian communications theorist and philosopher, Marshall McLuhan, wrote "the medium is the message," in which he meant that the medium itself was more important than the content of the messages it transmits.[29]

It had an immediate impact on the understanding of television's role in changing our economy. The signal of a local television station covered a larger geographic area than the customer base of many small businesses. They could not afford the cost of television advertising – local businesses like drug stores, department stores, men's and women's clothing stores, hardware stores, restaurants, even barber shops, were affected. The national chains had buying power that small businesses did not. They could not compete. Television destroyed many small businesses.

The franchise era was born where local businesses could buy a franchise for McDonalds, Burger King, Subway, Kentucky Fried Chicken, Dollar stores and others. National chains thrived. Big box stores crowded out the smaller neighborhood businesses. Lowes, Staples, Walmart, Amazon dominate.

National associations were formed to allow national advertising and local ownership, like True Value and Ace Hardware. The economic landscape had changed to favor

---

[29] Marshall McLuhan and Lewis Lapham, *Understanding Media: The Extensions of Man* (MIT Press), 1964), page 7.

national and international businesses.

To further understand the significance of McLuhan's insight, consider the "medium" of air conditioning. It was designed to cool homes, offices, manufacturing plants and cars. But it allowed hot Southern climates to air condition their offices, homes and industrial plants. It allowed businesses to move from the north to the south for lower wages and fewer unions. It changed the economy, where people lived and worked, where companies located their national headquarters.

The Eisenhower administration launched the interstate highway system. A part of its rationale was to be able to move military equipment and troops quickly and efficiently.

It also allowed the general public to move further faster. As a result, workers can get to their jobs in the cities more quickly and it allows them to move from the city to suburban areas. It facilitated the movement of goods long distances by truck. The truck eliminated the need to load and unload train cars. The "medium" of the highway system changed the economy and the lifestyles of the nation in many ways.

The same is true of every technological advance, whether it is the automobile, electricity, the internet or AI. Our world is in constant change – we are co-creators. We are change agents.

Personal Reflection & Notes:

TEN

GROUP CONVERSATION

Guidelines for Group Conversations

Small Group Conversations will help bring individuals into closer, deeper, and trusting relationships by sharing deep insights and experiences. The group may be a book club, congregational study group, or a board of directors of a community organization. Participants should have read the entire book prior to the discussion.

The group may want to agree to certain rules. Select a moderator for each session to ensure everyone is able to share. Meet in a room that is private. Form a circle where everyone can see and hear. Be aware that some people speak very softly. Encourage audible speech.

Agree that what is shared is confidential and will not leave the room. Speak in "I" statements representing you rather than your larger identity. Do not speak <u>over</u> another person. Allow time for each person to speak. Take time for group members to ask questions and fully explore the impact of the experience. Determine a start and ending time.

Session One:

Start with questions about the content of the book. Was there something you didn't quite understand? Do you accept the basic premise: our words can be incarnational and change someone's life, whether we know it or not?

Session Two:

Share childhood messages that may have been a script for your life. Both positive and negative. What were some traumas in your life that governed your thinking and behavior. What was your self-image at five, ten, fifteen?

Session Three:

Share any of your experiences that were incarnational and transformational that literally turned your life around into an entirely different direction. Teachers may have been the affirming, loving person. Elaborate on how you became a different person. Who was the person who most influenced your life? How? What stories of incarnational change affected you most deeply?

Session Four:

Share experiences where another person was changed by your words, an incarnational moment. What was their new direction. Did people notice? How did it affect their relationships?

Session Five:

How do you experience the power of love. Why do you think it's so difficult for you or others to tell family and friends, "I love you"?

How do we create a culture of love, if love is the "most powerful force in the universe?" Is it to encourage everyone to work to eradicate injustices, the isms, the "other" – to create King's **"Beloved Community?"** What other ways can you think of?

The moderator can help the group become more at ease in saying "I love you!" Have them turn to seat mates and say, "I love you" to at least three persons. Then ask them to all say together three times, "I LOVE YOU, I LOVE YOU, I LOVE YOU." Then ask them to repeat it again, three times, but louder.

Now quietly, take the hands of another, look them in the eye, and say "I Love You."

Lastly, let everyone say together, "let love flow through me." "Let love flow through you." Let love flow everywhere.

Close with, as we move from this place into our world, may our love be powerful. May we see love in others and may we see God's universal and creative love in people and nature all around us. Amen

If you think "Change Agent" can help create a more loving community, recommend it to others.

Personal Reflection & Notes:

BIBLIOGRAPHY

Acts 10:34, God's Word Translation, Bible Gateway, Accessed April 25, 2025, https://www.biblegateway.com/passage/?search=Acts%201 0%3A34-43&version=GW;NIV.

Barton, Ruth Haley. "Listening for the Divine Voice: Weekly Summary, *Center* for Action and Contemplation. October 26, 2024. https://cac.org/daily-meditations/listening-for-the-divine-voice-weekly-summary.

Bergoglio, Jorge Mario. "Encyclical Letter of the Holy Father Francis on The Human and Divine Love of the Heart of Jesus Christ." The Holy See, October 24, 2024. https://www.vatican.va/content/francesco/en/encyclicals/d ocuments /20241024-enciclica-dilexit-nos.html.

Bruesehoff, Jamie. *Raising Kids Beyond the Binary*. Broadleaf Books, 2023.

Charleston, Steven. *We Survived the End of the World.* Broadleaf Books, 2023.

Curry, Michael. *"Love Takes Commitment."* Center for Contemplation and Action. November 7, 2024. https://cac.org/daily-meditations/love-takes-commitment .

Deats, Richard. Martin Luther King, Jr. Spirit-Led Prophet. New City Press, 2000.

Delio, Ilia. "Christogenesis by Any Other Name?" Center for Christogenesis, October 12, 2020. https://christogenesis.org/christogenesis-by-any-other-name.

Editors of Encyclopedia Britannica. "Incarnation." Encyclopedia Britannica. April 30, 2025. https://www.britannica.com/topic/Christianity/The-problem-of-scriptural-authority.

General Commission on Archives and History, "John Wesley Speaks on Love," The United Methodist Church, 2025. https://www.umc.org/-/media/umc-media/2024/04/08/20/41/John%20Wesley%20on%20Love.pdf .

Haines, Errin. "Darnella Frazier, the Teen Who Filmed George Floyd's Murder, Wins Honorary Pulitzer." The 19th, The 19th News. June 11, 2021. https://19thnews.org/2021/06/darnella-frazier-teen-filmed-george-floyds-murder-wins-honorary-pulitzer.

Hanh, Thich Nat. *Your True Home: The Everyday Wisdom.* Shambala Publications Inc., 2011.

Iovino, Joe. "Holy Spirit Moments: Learning from Wesley at Aldersgate, The United Methodist Church, April 30, 2025.

https://www.umc.org/en/content/holy-spirit-moments-learning-from-wesley-at-aldersgate .

King, Jr. Center for Nonviolent Social Change, *"The King Philosophy – Nonviolence 365,"* The King Center, accessed April 29, 2025. https://thekingcenter.org/about-tkc/the-king-philosophy .

Logan, Ben, Ed. *Television Awareness Training.* Abingdon Press, 1979.

Love, Fr. John. Lecture at St. Lucy's Roman Catholic Church, Syracuse, N.Y., April 18, 2024.

McLuhan, Marshall and Lewis Lapham, *Understanding Media: The Extensions of Man.* MIT Press, 1964.

Obama, Michelle, *The Light We Carry.* Crown, 2022.

Plummer, Juliette. "The Transformational Power of Love in Hinduism," John Templeton Foundation, June 21, 2023. https://www.templeton.org/news/the-transformational-power-of-love-in-hinduism .

Rohr, Richard. *"Evolving Faithfully," Center* for Action and Contemplation. July 7, 2024. https://cac.org/daily-meditations/evolving-faithfully.

Rohr, Richard. The Universal Christ: How a Forgotten Reality Can Change Everything We See, Hope For, and Believe. Convergent Books, 2019.

Rowley, Richard, director/writer. *Documenting Hate: New American Nazis,* Season 2018, Episode 17, Frontline, PBS, November 3, 2020. https://www.youtube.com/watch?v=-XFBVAAzXjc.

Siracusa, Anthony. "Civil Rights Leader James Lawson, Who Learned from Gandhi, Used Nonviolent Resistance and the 'Power of Love' To Challenge Injustice." The Conversation, June 13, 2024. https://theconversation.com/civil-rights-leader-james-lawson-who-learned-from-gandhi-used-nonviolent-resistance-and-the-power-of-love-to-challenge-injustice-232232.

Tick, Edward. War and the Soul: Healing our Nation's Veterans from Post-traumatic Stress Disorder. Quest Books, 2005.

"Truth and Reconciliation Commission (South Africa)." Wikipedia. Wikimedia Foundation, Inc., March 2, 2025. https://en.wikipedia.org/wiki .

United Methodist Church. "Glossary: Wesleyan Quadrilateral." United Methodist Communications, April 15, 2025. https://www.umc.org/en/content/glossary-wesleyan-quadrilateral-the.

Wikimedia Foundation, Inc. 'Claudette Colvin.' April 10, 2025. https://en.wikipedia.org/wiki/Claudette_Colvin

ACKNOWLEDGMENTS

The examples of television, radio and educational programs are the products of creative and dedicated staff, colleagues, mentors, coalitions with leaders of other denominations and faiths.

My colleagues and I hired the most talented, skilled and smartest people we could find. It is their work that created events and programs that so powerfully affected peoples' lives.

While sailing on Lake Ontario, Robert and Louise Cannon – Bob & Lou -- we discussed my "incarnational" insight. They urged me to write about it. It took several years for me to do it. They were early readers of the manuscript. Copy editors. They tested the concept with three clergy in their area. The response was overwhelmingly positive and encouraging.

The Rev. Derek Van Gulden, pastor of First Congregational Church, Rockport, MA

The Rev. Sue Koehler-Arsenault, pastor, Annisquan Village Church, Gloucester, MA

The Rev. Mike Duda, senior pastor, First Church, Wenham, MA

Bob & Lou were change agents in my life, truly life changing.

Readers gave me feedback and ideas: My wife, Barbara Croll Fought was a reader, critic, editor, footnote creator and encourager. She helped me navigate the computer and the footnotes.

The Rev Dale Fryer was an early sceptic with many helpful suggestions.

Dara Moore helped the book be more inclusive to broaden its appeal. Donna Price was a reader and consultant.

Thank you to the contributors who shared their stories and life experiences.

Terry Hershey, his willingness to participate in this venture and write the foreword. He gave me encouragement in his weekly "Sabbath Moment" meditation when I heard him speaking directly to me, "Show your Light."

Roger L. Burgess changed my life's work and my life. Roger was a high school classmate, preacher's kid, and a year ahead of me at Morningside College in Sioux City, Iowa. When I arrived, he was managing editor of the college newsmagazine, and I became a reporter. As we moved through our college years, he became editor and when he graduated, I succeeded him. We did public relations for the college.

When Roger graduated, he took a job in Nashville, TN with the denomination's Methodist Youth Council. When I graduated, he recommended me for a pilot program: a communications specialist in a Methodist bishop's office. If successful, it would be rolled out across the country. It was successful.

Again, Roger recommended me for a job with the Television, Radio & Film Commission of the Methodist Church nationally. Our families remained friends through the years and the last five years with the Church, he was my boss as general secretary of United Methodist Communications. It was a full circle – the beginning in college – the end of my Methodist career.

The Church had its own titles for job positions. The top job was General Secretary. In the business world, it was president. Associate General Secretaries were heads of divisions, comparable to vice presidents. We remained friends until his and his wife's deaths.

Roger was a major change agent in my life.

Each of us is a change agent, whether we intend to be or not.

Terry Hershey

Terry Hershey is an author, humorist, inspirational speaker, dad, ordained minister, golf addict, and smitten by French wine. He divides his time between designing sanctuary gardens and sharing his practice of "pausing" and "sanctuary," to help us rest, renew, and live wholehearted. His work has been featured on The Hallmark Channel, PBS, and NPR. Terry holds a mirror up to our fast-forward, disconnected lives, and offers us the "power of pause"—the wisdom of doing less and living more– in order to regain emotional and spiritual balance;

to find the sacred in every day. Most days, you can find Terry out in his garden—on Vashon Island in the Puget Sound—because he believes that there is something fundamentally spiritual about dirt under your fingernails.

Workshop descriptions:

https://www.terryhershey.com/speaking/speaking-topics/

Sabbath Moment:

https://www.terryhershey.com/sabbath-moment/

Books:

https://www.terryhershey.com/product-category/books/

INDEXES

INDEX OF PEOPLE MENTIONED & CONTRIBUTORS

EVERYONE'S A CHANGE AGENT

NELSON PRICE

INDEX OF THEOLOGICAL REFERENCES

EVERYONE'S A CHANGE AGENT

For more information visit: NelsonPriceAuthor.com